OVERVIEW

Overview

Pablo is a hard worker who is respected by his boss and colleagues. But he has one problem that's holding him back in his career – his complete lack of organization. He often loses important documents in the clutter on his desk, and is frequently late to meetings because he can't find what he needs to prepare. The clutter makes it hard for Pablo to concentrate on his job. Even worse, he leaves a poor first impression, which he's convinced is the reason he hasn't been promoted.

Does Pablo's situation sound familiar? Do you ever feel the same way? Or maybe you're not nearly as disorganized as he is, but you know someone who is. Nearly everyone has dealt with workplace clutter at one time or another. If you have, you know that it can range from mildly annoying to practically paralyzing. Either way, clutter can have a serious, negative impact on productivity.

That's why dealing with clutter is so important. Removing the mess from your workspace and getting organized can significantly improve many aspects of your work day, including your ability to concentrate, achieve targets, and become more efficient.

This course will help you increase your productivity by showing you how to organize and maintain both your physical and digital workspace. First, you'll find out about the benefits of managing your workspace. You'll learn how creating a clutter-free workspace and effective filing can improve your productivity. But it's not just your physical workspace that needs decluttering – this course will show you how to manage digital files, which is just as important. Finally, you'll learn how to maintain an organized workspace.

The last time you were faced with a list of tasks, which one did you attend to first? Was it the most difficult? Was it a random choice, or did you choose the easiest task first? The latter points toward procrastination – a habit that sees urgent and difficult tasks pile up as you avoid them.

Procrastinators typically focus on the reasons not to do something, rather than just doing it. This undesirable quality can in turn produce undesirable consequences in the workplace.

Failure to submit important work on time leads to procrastinators being viewed as unprofessional and unreliable.

Procrastination is integrally linked to disorganization. Working in a disorganized fashion makes it almost impossible to function in a timely manner. For instance, think about the time wasted looking for a single document on a disorganized desktop. Organization can save you that time.

Personal Productivity Improvement

Wishing for more time is only wasting your time. Many procrastinators waste hours thinking about how they don't have time to work, rather than just working.

But focusing on saving time is missing the point. You have to invest time to gain more time later. Spending a morning planning the week ahead can lead to much more time being freed up later on.

Don't think about working more hours, think about working better hours. All workers would like to increase their productivity, but this doesn't necessarily mean more hours. Instead, use your time to get organized and avoid procrastination.

Throughout this course you'll learn how to avoid procrastination by becoming organized. The benefits of this are explained, as well as the causes of procrastination. Discipline is vital to overcoming procrastination, so the development of self-discipline is addressed. Finally, you'll learn how to set your priorities and know when to say "yes" to a new task and when to say "no."

The relationship between time and productivity has always fascinated people. Ancient cultures developed systems for marking the time for planting and harvesting by observing the relative positions of the sun, moon, and stars. In the Middle Ages, clocks were developed that tolled on the hour, publicly demarcating the workday. In the modern world, electronic timekeeping devices divide our workday into minutes, seconds, and even milliseconds.

But whether you count it in seasons, days, minutes, or seconds, the amount of time available to you is constant. You can't buy more time or trade it for another resource. You can't save it for later. But what you can do is increase your productivity – the value you produce in the time you have. And the better you understand your own personal productivity, the easier it will be to manage your time effectively.

In this course you'll learn about managing tasks in a way that maximizes your productivity. You'll discover the benefits of setting goals and how productivity is tied to your ability to assess time and set priorities. You'll learn about the process of "chunking" your time and the principles of efficient scheduling. You'll also learn about the different types of to-do lists, and how to use them effectively.

CHAPTER 1 - Managing Your Workspace

Section 1 - Benefits of Managing Your Workspace

Personal productivity

Pablo is a legal assistant at a large law firm. His boss asked him to prepare a report by the end of the day. With only an hour to go, Pablo is still frantically searching for a document he needs to finish the report. He's looked everywhere – in the piles of paper on his desk, in the disorganized files in his cabinet, and even in the recycling bin under his desk.

Finally, he locates the document and finishes the report with only minutes to spare. Pablo is relieved, but also stressed out. He was lucky this time – he found the document. But next time, he might not be so fortunate.

When you think of personal productivity, you probably don't think of a situation like Pablo's. Personal productivity is basically performing tasks that bring you closer to achieving your goals. This could involve goal setting, finishing projects, or managing your time better. And yes, you can do this with minimal stress.

The key to being productive is organization. When you work in an office, your workspace is central to everything you do.

It's easy enough to tidy your workspace every now and then. But if you want to consistently keep your workspace free of clutter, it's important that you understand the benefits of doing so.

Question

Take a moment to consider your current workspace. How would you rate it in terms of organization and functionality?

Options:

1. It's highly organized and I can always find what I need

2. It's slightly organized, but things sometimes get misplaced

3. It's very unorganized and I'm often searching for things

Answer

Option 1: It's great that your workspace is so organized! You probably enjoy the benefits of having an efficient workspace. Nevertheless, there's always room for improvement, and this course will give you some new ideas to manage your physical and digital workspaces, and to keep them organized.

Option 2: It's pretty common to occasionally lose track of items or documents in your workspace, so you're not alone. Taking this course will help you more effectively manage your physical and digital workspaces, and keep them organized.

Personal Productivity Improvement

Option 3: As you probably know, a disorganized workspace can have negative effects on your personal productivity. Whether you've tried to get organized in the past or have never attempted it, this course will give you the tools you need to more effectively manage your physical and digital workspaces and keep them organized.

Managing your workspace

Managing your workspace

Pablo found that effectively managing his workspace benefited him in four ways. It projects professionalism, decreases stress, improves his outlook, and increases productivity.

The first benefit of managing your workspace effectively is that it projects professionalism. The most successful people are usually the most organized because good skills in this area help them get more done. Being organized can also help you progress professionally.

First impressions matter, and your workspace is often the first impression your colleagues and clients have of you.

Would you rather project an image of having it organized, or of being overwhelmed and unable to handle your workload?

Your work might be impeccable, but a messy workspace sends a different message.

Another benefit of managing your workspace is that it decreases stress. A disorganized workspace can make you feel that you don't have your work under control. And this can increase your stress levels.

Imagine a workday where you never have to search for an important document and you're always prepared for meetings because you can find everything you need to bring. This type of day is the result of an organized workspace.

When you reduce stress caused by disorganization, you get better results in the workplace. Since you're no longer wasting time looking for things you've misplaced, you can focus on excelling at your job.

Managing your workspace more effectively can improve your outlook. Your desk is the first thing you see when you arrive at work and, if you work in an office, you spend many hours there each day. The state of your workspace can have a big influence on your daily outlook on life. A disorganized space can lead to feelings of frustration, helplessness, and irritation. A tidy, organized space, on the other hand, can significantly boost your mood and improve your state of mind.

In your response, you might have mentioned that an organized workspace can save you time. And that's true – managing your workspace effectively increases your productivity, which saves you time.

So what does an organized workspace look like? Ideally, you have plenty of desk space and file cabinet storage. Arrange things so that you know where everything is and can easily find items at a moment's notice.

Your space should also be comfortable. This means a workspace that's set up to be ergonomic and supportive.

Your time is valuable. Every minute spent searching through a disorganized space is time that could be used to advance your career.

Taking the time now to organize your space – and keep it organized – can have a positive impact on your long-term productivity. And an organized space can contribute to peace of mind, knowing that everything can be easily located. Without the anxiety of disorganization, you can spend your time being productive, not overwhelmed.

Question

Jody has been working hard to get rid of the collection of clutter she has amassed in her office. It's been a long process, but she's finally organized.

How might Jody benefit from managing her workspace effectively?

Options:

1. Her clients and colleagues will perceive her in a more professional way

2. She won't feel as stressed out as she did when her office was a mess

3. She'll feel confident and positive when she arrives at work each morning

4. She'll be able to complete a proposal she's been neglecting because she couldn't find the information she needed

5. Her boss will appreciate how productive she is now that her space is organized, and offer her a promotion she's been hoping for

6. She'll be able to get rid of a pile of old files that she doesn't want to deal with

Answer

Option 1: This option is correct. Managing your workspace effectively projects professionalism. Opinions are often based on first impressions. If your workspace is untidy, clients and colleagues may question your professionalism.

Option 2: This option is correct. When you feel out of control, your stress levels increase, and a disorganized workspace adds to this feeling. Effectively managing your workspace can help decrease your stress levels, leaving you more relaxed and able to focus on your job.

Option 3: This option is correct. Managing your workspace more effectively can improve your outlook. If a messy desk or office is the first thing that greets you in the morning, it's hard to have a positive outlook.

Option 4: This option is correct. Managing your workspace effectively can increase your productivity, which saves you time. When you waste time searching through a disorganized space, you don't have time to work on tasks that could possibly advance your career.

Option 5: This option is incorrect. Although effectively managing your workspace can increase your productivity, there's no guarantee it will lead to a promotion.

Option 6: This option is incorrect. Sorting through files may be part of effectively managing your workspace, but you still need to deal with them. Instead of tossing them out, though, you should figure out a good organizing system.

Section 2 - Managing Your Physical Workspace

A productive workspace

A productive workspace

When you think of a typical workspace, what comes to mind? You probably imagine a room or cubicle, maybe with a few filing cabinets or shelves. There's likely a desk covered in papers with a computer on it. Your own workspace may very well resemble this. But this doesn't exemplify good workspace management. Effective workspace management means starting from the biggest areas – the filing system or shelves and working your way down to the smallest – the digital filing system on your computer.

A productive workspace is minimalist, with no visual distractions. It has usable desk space and everything is within an arm's reach. Finally, it has neatly organized shelving and filing systems.

Minimalist

Sorin Dumitrascu

A tidy workspace is minimalist. You should get rid of as many extra items in your space as possible. Extra items mean clutter, and clutter leads to distraction. Keep only the things that are necessary.

Usable desk space

Usable desk space means just that – space on your desk you can actually use. You can't use your desk if it's covered in paper and files, so clear it off to give yourself room to work.

Everything within arm's reach

When everything you use regularly is within arm's reach, you'll avoid getting out of your chair to retrieve them. Not only does this waste time, but it also interrupts your work. When everything you need is close at hand, you'll be more productive.

By keeping frequently used paperwork and correspondence close at hand, they'll be easier to get to when you need them.

Neatly organized

It's easy to be productive when you have neatly organized shelves and filing systems. You might benefit from clearly labeled color-coded hanging folders or a small file box on your desk for frequently used items. It's also useful to organize books in alphabetical order and use bins to organize smaller items.

Consider Jorge, an accountant at an accounting firm. He's always jokingly described himself as an organized slob – even though his office was a mess, he could quickly locate anything. However, Jorge is hoping for a promotion, and his boss has hinted that his messy office doesn't project an image of a competent accountant. So, Jorge has decided to get organized once and for all.

Personal Productivity Improvement

The first thing he does is get rid of everything he doesn't need. He tosses old memos, take-out menus, and newsletters – anything that's not required to do his job.

Next, Jorge gets to work on his desk. He clears everything off, and the only things that go back on are his computer, a small desktop filing system, and a printer.

Jorge has a large filing cabinet in his office, as well as a small bookshelf. Although he can generally locate files, he knows his current system doesn't really make sense. He organizes his files alphabetically by client name, making it easier for himself and his assistants to retrieve files quickly.

He takes all the books off his bookshelf, and replaces only the reference books he uses regularly.

When Jorge is finished, he's quite happy with the results. But when he goes to grab a book, he realizes his bookshelf isn't within reach of his desk. He adjusts the furniture in his office, placing the bookshelf nearer to his desk so everything is close at hand.

Question

Margo feels that her workspace isn't as efficient as it could be. Her desk has her computer on it, as well as several photos, knick knacks, and plants, but the remainder of the desk is clear. The filing cabinet and shelving are far away from the desk. The bookcase is cluttered and disorganized. On the floor beside the desk, there is a small file box labeled "Correspondence."

What aspects of Margo's workspace make it unproductive?

Options:
1. The filing cabinet is too far away from the desk
2. There is too much visual distraction
3. The bookcase is too messy and disorganized

4. There is no usable desk space

5. Frequently used correspondence is too far away

Answer

Option 1: This option is correct. Everything you use regularly should be within arm's reach so you can avoid having to get out of your chair to retrieve them.

Option 2: This option is correct. A productive workspace is minimalist, so get rid of as many extra items in your space as possible, keeping only the things that are necessary.

Option 3: This option is correct. Messy and disorganized shelves and filing systems make it difficult to be productive.

Option 4: This option is incorrect. Actually, Margo has plenty of usable desk space – it just has unnecessary items on it.

Option 5: This option is incorrect. Margo's correspondence is actually close at hand, which is a good way to be more productive.

Creating a clutter-free workspace

Creating a clutter-free workspace

A clutter-free workspace can be one of the best ways to increase your productivity. Getting organized and staying that way might not be easy, but it can have significant benefits.

Question

Think about how you currently manage your workspace. Is it something you do often or only once in awhile?

Options:

1. I rarely organize my workspace
2. I tidy up once in awhile
3. I organize my workspace every day

Answer

Option 1: If you only organize your workspace when you reach the point where you can't find anything, you probably feel frustrated at the work involved. Managing your workspace should be a continuous process, not an event. This topic will outline some techniques for improving your skills in this area.

Option 2: Tidying up when your office starts to get messy probably keeps you from being completely overwhelmed by the task. However, managing your workspace is even easier when it's a continuous process – not an event. This topic will show you a few techniques to improve your skills in this area.

Option 3: It's great that you organize your workspace every day before you leave work. You know that managing your workspace is a continuous process, not an event. This topic will reinforce your good habits, as well as show you a few new techniques to improve your skills in this area.

Unless you're diligent about keeping your work area tidy, things can quickly pile up. But if you manage your physical workspace well, you can avoid the frustration that goes along with disorganization. There are three steps you can take to more effectively manage your physical workspace. You should visualize what you want to achieve and set goals; organize one area at a time; and go through clutter and address paper overload.

The first step is to visualize what you want to achieve and set goals. Close your eyes and picture your ideal workspace. What do you need in the space to be productive? Where will you keep your current work? What kind of filing system would be most useful?

Now that you have a clear idea of what you want your space to look like, it's time to set goals to help achieve your vision.

Personal Productivity Improvement

For example, you might decide that one of your goals is to be able to clear your in-box in half an hour each day. Or maybe one of your goals is to stop missing deadlines due to disorganization.

Bart is an executive at a computer software company. In the past, he has always waited until his office was so messy he couldn't stand it. Then he would spend an entire day tidying up. He's decided that maintaining an organized space would be much more efficient, and is clearing out the clutter.

Bart determines that his ideal workspace is an office that has no clutter and is neatly organized. His goals are to clear off his desk every night before he leaves, and to have only one location for all his project files.

Once you've decided what you want to achieve and have set some goals, you can begin organizing. But don't just jump in and throw random pieces of paper in the trash. It's important to organize only one area at a time, which is the second step in the process. Be sure to start with the area that bothers you the most.

Starting with a small area is a great way to stay motivated because you'll get immediate results without becoming overwhelmed.

It's easy to become discouraged when you try to do everything at once, and may decide it's not worth the effort.

Remember Bart? When he starts organizing his office, he begins with his desk. He clears off several piles of paper, file folders, coffee cups, and old newspapers. Then, he puts his laptop back on the desk, along with his phone and an external hard drive that he uses daily.

Question

Jasmine is an administrative assistant at a pharmaceutical company. Her boss has asked her to organize her messy workspace because it doesn't leave a good first impression with clients.

What actions should Jasmine take first to create a clutter-free workspace?

Options:

1. She imagines a reception area that's tidy and welcoming

2. She decides that her goal is to be able to find client files in her filing cabinet within one minute

3. She focuses first on her client files because they cause her the most frustration

4. She takes everything off her shelves, desk, and filing cabinet so she can organize everything at one time

5. She starts organizing by jumping right in – she figures she'll come up with a plan as she goes

Answer

Option 1: This option is correct. One of the first steps in creating a clutter-free workspace is to visualize what you want to achieve by imagining your ideal workspace.

Option 2: This option is correct. When creating a clutter-free workspace, one of the first steps is to set goals to achieve your vision for your ideal workspace.

Option 3: This option is correct. You can start organizing once you've decided what you want to achieve and have set goals. It's important to organize only one area at a time, starting with the area that bothers you the most.

Option 4: This option is incorrect. When you begin organizing, it's important to start with only one area at a time. If you try to do everything at once, you'll probably become discouraged and stop altogether.

Option 5: This option is incorrect. Before you start organizing, it's important to visualize what you want to achieve and set goals to achieve your vision.

The final step in creating a clutter-free workspace is to go through clutter and address paper overload. Most people have some sort of clutter in their offices – work-related and otherwise. Be sure to take home any non-work related belongings so they're not cluttering your workspace.

Paper clutter is very common. When you sort through the paper from your desk or drawers, be ruthless! Did you know that 80% of the paper saved "just in case" is never used again? It can be hard to decide what to do with paper, so use these guidelines for each piece of paper: discard it, pass it along, file it, or take action.

Discard it

If you can't think of any good reason to keep a particular piece of paper, the best place for it is the recycling bin. Toss away those old newspapers, magazines, memos you printed months ago, and catalogs you'll never order from. If you discard something you later need, you'll likely be able to get another copy.

Pass it along

If you pick up a piece of paper and determine that someone else should be taking care of it, pass it along. Delegating tasks that can or should be done by someone else is one of the keys to personal productivity. Perhaps you have no idea what to do with a paper, but know that someone else in the department could make a decision. In this case as well, pass it along.

File it

Sometimes you'll come across a piece of paper that you don't need now but will need in the future. You can file these away. But keep in mind that the majority of papers that are filed are never needed again. Before you file something, ask yourself what would happen if you couldn't find it again. If the answer is "nothing," you should discard it.

Take action

Some pieces of paper require that you take action, such as letters, proposals, and messages that need a decision. It's a good idea to create a file labeled "Action" and place it where you will see it.

When he's decluttering the paper in his office, Bart finds an old sales report that he's unsure about. What if he needs to reference the figures again? But after a few moments' consideration, Bart puts it in the recycling bin. He knows his company keeps a digital copy of all reports and, if he ever needs the information, he'll be able to access it.

As he goes through his papers, Bart comes across a document containing a list of possible sales leads. He passes it along to the head of the Sales Department, who normally takes care of this type of task.

Bart also finds a large pile of business cards collected over the years. He wants to keep these, since they could be important contacts, so he creates a file for business contacts. When he finds a proposal that he needs to read through and sign, he places it in his "Action" file so he'll remember to do it before the end of the day.

Question

Personal Productivity Improvement

As Jasmine, an administrative assistant, declutters her workspace, she comes across many pieces of paper that she needs to deal with.

Determine what Jasmine should do with each piece of paper by matching the type of paper to the appropriate action.

Options:

A. A menu from a restaurant that has closed

B. A pile of payroll information that the accountant needs

C. A document containing client information that she frequently refers to

D. A contract with a new courier that requires her to sign and fax back

Targets:

1. Discard it
2. Pass it along
3. File it
4. Take action

Answer

A menu from a closed restaurant is an example of a paper that should be put in the recycling bin. If you can't think of any good reason to keep a piece of paper, the best place for it is the recycling bin.

A pile of payroll information needed by the accountant is an example of paper that you should pass along. If you pick up a piece of paper and determine that someone else should be taking care of it, pass it along.

A document containing client information that's frequently referred to is an example of a paper that you should file or archive. If you come across a piece of paper that you don't need now but will need in the future, you can file it away.

A contract with a new courier that requires a signature and to be sent back is an example of a paper that requires you to take action. Some pieces of paper require that you take action, such as letters, proposals, and messages that need a decision, and it's a good idea to create a file labeled "Action" and place it where you will see it.

Effective filing

Effective filing

Once you've decluttered your workspace, you should organize everything that you've kept. Developing an effective filing system that encompasses all your work enables you to find things when they're needed.

One of the most effective ways to organize your files is by frequency of use – in other words, how often they're needed. Think of your desk as a work surface. The only papers on it should be the ones you're currently working with. Stacks of papers on your desk aren't efficient, so clear these away.

Your files should be divided into three main categories: active files, reference files, and permanent or archived files.

Active files

Active or working files are your current working projects and the administrative tasks you perform regularly. For example, an active file might contain phone lists, computer codes, or company information you access regularly.

Reference files

Reference files are those that aren't used as frequently as active files, but might be required on a monthly basis. These include research for future projects, personnel information, client account records, and past projects you might need to refer to.

Permanent or archived files

Permanent or archived files are rarely referenced, and it could be years before they're needed. Each company sets up its archive differently, but it's important that everyone in the company knows how to use it.

When you're setting up your filing system, you should follow the principles of effective filing: sort by like and consolidate files; don't use fancy file labeling; and purge files regularly.

Sort by like and consolidate files

The best way to deal with files is to sort them into basic general categories. You might begin by sorting paper into groups on your desk, and identifying patterns that emerge.

For instance, suppose you notice three general categories – your company's five-year plan, your department's five-year plan, and a copy of your company's annual goals. These can all be consolidated into one file labeled with your company's name and "Planning."

Don't use fancy file labeling

Label your files using common sense and file them alphabetically. Besides organizing them in alphabetical order, there are numerous other ways you can categorize files, including by subject, numerically, geographically, and chronologically.

It's also useful to label files with nouns. For example, a label titled "Contract Negotiations" makes more sense than "How to Negotiate Contracts."

Finally, label files according to how you use information, not where you found it. For instance, if you regularly save articles from newsletters or magazines, file them according to the subject of the article, not the name of the source.

Purge files regularly

No matter how organized your files are, you still need to purge them regularly by getting rid of the information you no longer need. This includes current files, reference files, and archive files. Purging files makes it easier to maintain a clutter-free filing system, keeping only the things that are truly required.

No matter what you ultimately decide to do with paper clutter, turning each piece into an action item is an important step in maintaining a productive workspace.

Deal with each piece of paper before it has the chance to become clutter. If you come back from a conference with a pile of business cards, either deal with them immediately or put them into an action folder.

The same principle applies to every piece of paper you encounter. If you can't action it immediately, figure out what steps you need to take to deal with it before it ends up in a pile on your desk.

Question

Jasmine, an administrative assistant, needs to set up an effective filing system to deal with the paper in her workspace.

Which of Jasmine's actions are examples of the principles of effective filing?

Options:

1. She identifies two main piles of paper – customer contact information and customer purchases – which she groups into consolidated files by customer name
2. When filing information about suppliers, she labels the files with only the company's name
3. She determines that she will go through working files monthly to get rid of unimportant information
4. She files customer information by last name and supplier information by account number
5. She places archived files in a box and stores them in a closet, happy she no longer has to deal with them

Answer

Option 1: This option is correct. The best way to deal with files is to sort them into basic general categories.

Option 2: This option is correct. Files should be labeled using common sense and organized alphabetically. The company's name is the most logical way to file supplier information.

Option 3: This option is correct. Purging files makes it easier to maintain a clutter-free filing system, keeping only the things that are truly required.

Option 4: This option is incorrect. You should label your files using common sense and file them alphabetically. Filing customer information alphabetically and supplier information numerically isn't logical.

Option 5: This option is incorrect. You need to purge all files, including archived files, regularly to maintain a clutter-free filing system.

Section 3 - Managing Your Digital Workspace

Managing digital files

Managing digital files

How many times have you had to locate a document on your computer or e-mail something only to discover that it was lost somewhere deep within your hard drive?

Even if you can usually find things on your computer, it's important to remember that your computer is a key part of your workspace. Keeping it in order is just as essential as keeping your physical workspace tidy and organized.

Using your computer for filing can benefit you in several ways. Digital information is much easier to store, manipulate, receive, and transmit than traditional paper files. In fact, many offices are increasingly using less paper, going digital wherever possible. With such a large number of electronic tools available, it makes sense to do away with paper when you can.

Personal Productivity Improvement

If a near-paperless office is your goal, you need to convert paper documents into an electronic format. But going digital isn't a magic formula for getting rid of clutter – be careful that you don't fall into the trap of using digital documents as a to-do list by gathering files that represent the tasks you need to do. A cluttered computer can lower your productivity just as much as a cluttered office.

You can increase your productivity by practicing good digital file management techniques. First, mirror your paper filing system in your computer's filing system. Be sure to use consistent, logical file names. You should use versioning in your digital files. Finally, organize desktop files by creating a desktop system that makes filing and organizing easy.

Mirror paper filing system

You wouldn't dump files randomly into a filing cabinet, and you shouldn't do it with your computer files either. The best way to organize digital files is to think of your computer as an electronic filing cabinet and mirror your paper filing system. You should set up general categories, group applications and files, and subcategorize. This will make it easier to quickly find what you're looking for.

You can organize your files in the way that makes most sense for you. For instance, your file categories could include projects, customers, content, or date.

Use consistent, logical names

When setting up your digital filing system, use consistent, logical naming for ease of file retrieval. Just as you would with paper files, use nouns for names – for instance, Archives, Invoices, and Taxes.

To reduce the time it takes to find documents when you need them, use file names that make the most sense to you. A file's title should make it absolutely clear what it contains. For example, if you have a number of documents relating to your vehicle – such as warranty and finance information – the most logical file name would be simply "Car."

Use versioning

Versioning is a great way to keep track of documents and ensure you can always find the most recent version. The file name should make the version of a document clear. If you're updating a file named "Property Management Report," you should name the new copy "Property Management Report: Version 2" so you can easily find the most recent document.

Organize desktop files

To enhance productivity, make sure your computer's desktop doesn't resemble an electronic to-do list – it shouldn't be a repository for every document you're currently working on. Instead, your desktop system should be set up to make filing and organizing easy.

For example, you might start by creating three folders: working, reference, and archive. Then, you can organize files within these folders according to their importance.

It's important to note that your files must be backed up before you begin deleting folders and reorganizing documents. You can back up your files on an external hard drive, CD, or server, but remember – failing to back up your data files can lead to big problems.

Question

Taku is a professor at a university. He wants to set up a more efficient system for managing his digital files.

What are examples of techniques Taku can use to manage his digital files?

Personal Productivity Improvement

Options:

1. He sets up a filing system for student information that resembles the one he uses for nondigital information

2. He creates folders for student information and labels each with the student's name

3. He renames a research paper with the most recent version number each time he updates it

4. He clears all icons off his computer's desktop and replaces them with folders that make organizing class lectures easier

5. He creates folders for each student, labeling some with the student's name and others with the student's ID number

6. He keeps links to all his active documents on his computer's desktop

Answer

Option 1: This option is correct. The best way to organize digital files is to mirror your paper filing system. You can do this by setting up general categories, grouping applications and files, and subcategorizing them so you can quickly find what you need.

Option 2: This option is correct. When you set up your digital filing system, you should use consistent, logical naming for ease of file retrieval.

Option 3: This option is correct. Versioning is a way you can keep track of documents and ensure you can always find the most recent version. The file name should make the version of a document clear, and you should update it each time you make changes to the document.

Option 4: This option is correct. Your computer's desktop shouldn't contain every document you're working on. Instead, it should be set up to make filing and organizing easy.

Option 5: This option is incorrect. Actually, when you set up your digital filing system, you should use consistent, logical naming for ease of file retrieval.

Option 6: This option is incorrect. Your computer's desktop should be set up to make filing and organizing easy, and keeping links to every document you're working on isn't efficient.

Managing e-mail

Managing e-mail

The number of e-mails received can be overwhelming. When you take control of your e-mail, your productivity will increase. You'll be better able to stay on top of deadlines. It can even improve customer relationships, since you'll no longer miss important e-mails.

Generally speaking, e-mails typically fall into one of two categories: active or permanent.

Active e-mails require action on your part. These include unanswered e-mails, unpaid bills, and those that are awaiting a reply.

Permanent e-mails, on the other hand, are those that should be filed away for reference. Paid bills, answered e-mails, and anything else you want to keep but don't need to take action on are all permanent e-mails.

In fact, e-mail is similar to any paper or electronic file when it comes to management. The four-step process you use to deal with e-mails is the same as for paper documents: you either discard it, pass it along to someone else, file it, or take action. If you don't take care of e-mails as soon as you open them, they'll probably sit in your inbox. Deal with each e-mail only once, preferably as soon as you read it.

Keeping your e-mail under control doesn't have to be complicated. You can use three techniques to better manage it: manage your inbox, file or archive on your hard drive, and take control of spam.

Manage your inbox

If you want to take control of your e-mail, it's essential that you manage your inbox methodically and regularly. As with any organizing project, if you practice routine management, you won't be overwhelmed. A good way to stay on top of it is to regularly delete unwanted e-mails. Make a decision as you read each one, and delete it if it has no value. You have to be ruthless – if you can't think of a reason to keep an e-mail, delete it.

A common reason people avoid deleting e-mail is that they doubt themselves, thinking they may need to read a message again in the future. To stop this self-doubt, turn off the prompt that asks if you're sure you want to permanently delete a message. Another good way of managing e-mail is to screen messages using the subject line. You should be able to immediately determine if a message is important simply by reading the subject line.

File or archive

Mail shouldn't be stored within your inbox; instead, you should create a filing system for e-mails you wish to keep. Set up folders within your e-mail system so they mirror your paper filing system, and transfer e-mails you want to keep into their appropriate folders.

When you're naming folders, use logical file names so e-mails can easily be located when you need to reference them. And of course, the folders will be useless if you don't actually use them! Get in the habit of transferring e-mails to their appropriate folders as soon as you've read them so they don't pile up in your inbox.

Take control of spam

If you use e-mail, you've undoubtedly encountered spam. These messages can take up a lot of your time if you don't manage them, so it's important to take steps to stop spam.

One of the best ways to deal with spam is to use an effective Internet service provider – or ISP – to block it. It's also worthwhile to invest in a powerful spam blocker. And don't forget to set the security on your e-mail to its highest level.

Consider Travis. He's a senior executive and receives over 200 e-mails a day. His inbox contains well over 1,000 messages and he is finding it increasingly difficult to keep track of what is important. The first thing Travis does is open each message. He makes an immediate decision on each one and deletes any message that contains information he doesn't need or that could be easily found elsewhere.

Next, Travis sets up an e-mail filing system. He creates folders for e-mails that require action, reference e-mails that contain useful information but don't require action, and permanent e-mails that he won't need to refer to often.

Finally, Travis deals with spam. He knows he's let his anti-spam software expire, so he renews his subscription.

He also does a bit of research and switches to an ISP that has much better service in terms of blocking spam.

Case Study: Question 1 of 2

Scenario

Imagine that your e-mail inbox is so full that you're becoming overwhelmed. You must implement ways to manage your e-mail more effectively.

Answer the questions in order.

Question

Your inbox is full because you haven't been managing your e-mail regularly. You tend to keep many messages "just in case." You're also inundated with e-mail from unwanted sources, and dealing with these takes up a lot of your time.

What actions can you take to reduce the size of your disorganized inbox and improve your productivity?

Options:

1. Set your e-mail program to stop asking if you're certain you to want to delete an e-mail

2. Go through each e-mail and ask yourself if the information it contains has any value – if it doesn't, you delete it

3. Have your company purchase and install a powerful spam blocking program on your computer

4. Set up a filing system within your e-mail program to sort and organize messages

5. Delete all e-mail messages that have been in your inbox for a year or longer

Answer

Option 1: This option is correct. If you want to take control of your e-mail, manage your inbox methodically and regularly. One way to do this is to stop doubting yourself and turn off the prompt that asks if you're sure you want to permanently delete a message.

Option 2: This option is correct. It's essential that you manage your inbox if you want to avoid being overwhelmed by e-mail. A good way to stay on top of it is to regularly delete unwanted e-mails by reading each one and deleting it if it has no value.

Option 3: This option is correct. Spam can take up a lot of time and inbox space if you don't manage it. A good way to stop spam is to invest in a powerful spam blocker.

Option 4: This option is incorrect. Before you organize your e-mail messages, you first need to manage your inbox by deleting messages and dealing with spam problems.

Option 5: This option is incorrect. Although deleting messages is an important part of e-mail management, some messages should be kept for reference. You shouldn't delete a message without first reading it to determine if it contains important information.

Case Study: Question 2 of 2

You've gone through your entire inbox and have deleted all the e-mails that you no longer need. You've also addressed unwanted e-mails that arrive in the form of spam. However, you still have a few hundred e-mails that you need to keep, but regularly have to sort through to find what you need.

What actions can you take to deal with your overflowing inbox?

Options:

1. Set up folders within your e-mail program to organize old messages
2. Name the folders you create "Customer invoices," "Reference materials," and "Pending"
3. Continue deleting messages until you feel your inbox is at a manageable level
4. Create a folder within your e-mail program titled "Archived e-mail" to store all the messages you want to keep but don't need at present

Answer

Option 1: This option is correct. E-mail shouldn't be stored in your inbox, so it's a good idea to create a filing system for messages you wish to keep. The folders you create should mirror your paper filing system, and you transfer e-mails you want to keep into the appropriate folders.

Option 2: This option is correct. When you're naming folders, be sure to use logical file names so e-mails can easily be located when you need to reference them.

Option 3: This option is incorrect. When you have messages you need to keep, you should create a filing system to organize them. Set up folders so they mirror your paper filing system, and transfer e-mails you want to keep into their appropriate folders.

Option 4: This option is incorrect. Although you should create a filing system to organize messages you need to keep, using only one folder isn't effective. Instead, you should create a filing system that mirrors your paper filing system so messages will be easy to retrieve.

Section 4 - Maintaining an Organized Workspace

Handling items and filing

Handling items and filing

Getting organized will benefit you in many ways – you'll probably be more productive, you'll feel more confident, and your colleagues are more likely to think highly of you. But getting organized is just half the battle. If you want to keep enjoying all those benefits, you must continually manage your workspace once it's been decluttered.

You can use four techniques to help you manage an organized workspace. These are handling each item as it comes in, keeping filing systems up to date, forming the habit of clearing your desk each night, and adding notes where they belong.

The first technique for maintaining an organized workspace is to handle each item as it comes in. If you aren't careful, stacks of paper can quickly pile up. For example, Cathy, an executive assistant, keeps all her papers in a filing cabinet, in hanging folders so they don't pile up on her desk.

However, a filing cabinet won't be very useful if you don't actually use it. To ensure that your papers don't get out of control, take immediate action on each piece of paper, as well as every digital file, as it comes into your workspace.

Don't put a paper in a pile to be dealt with later – handle each piece only once. Deciding what to do with it right away means you won't have to come back to it later, saving you valuable time.

It's important to have an organized place to put papers. That's why it's essential that you keep paper and digital filing systems up to date. For instance, Cathy, the executive assistant, regularly goes through her paper and digital files, consolidating those that overlap, eliminating files that are no longer needed, and creating new categories when needed. Keeping your files up to date means you'll never have to search through piles of paper to find what you need.

For optimal maintenance, you should deal with your files daily, weekly, and monthly. Every day, Cathy ensures that her desk is clear of papers by filing them appropriately.

Each week, Cathy transfers projects she's completed into the filing cabinet. If you have an action folder of work you need to complete, go through this to determine if any of the items can be filed away.

Finally, at the end of the month, Cathy browses through her filing cabinet and gets rid of any files she no longer needs.

Question

Addison has worked hard to get her office decluttered and organized. Now she wants to maintain her workspace.

Match the techniques Addison can use to maintain an organized space to their appropriate examples. Each technique will match to more than one example.

Options:

A. Handle each item as it comes in

B. Keep filing systems up to date

Targets:

1. She opens her mail immediately each day, tossing out junk mail and either filing or putting important papers into an action folder

2. When she receives a memo or other document that requires her attention, she deals with it immediately

3. She sorts through her filing cabinet at the end of each month, discarding any information she no longer needs

4. She finds several files that contain similar information, and consolidates them into one folder

Answer

Opening mail every day and filing documents immediately is an example of handling each item as it comes in. To ensure that papers don't get out of control, take immediate action on each item as it comes into your workspace.

Dealing with papers as soon as you receive them is an example of handling each item as it comes in. Papers can get out of control quickly, so take immediate action on each item.

Going through your filing cabinet once a month is an example of keeping filing systems up to date. When you keep files up to date, you'll never have to search through piles of paper to find what you need.

Consolidating files is an example of keeping filing systems up to date. A good way to do this is to go through files, consolidating those that overlap, eliminating files that are no longer needed, and creating new categories when needed.

Clearing your desk and making notes

Clearing your desk and making notes

The third technique for maintaining an organized workspace is forming a habit of clearing your desk every night. When the first thing you encounter upon entering your office is a messy desk, it's difficult to be productive for the rest of the day. A clean desk means a clean slate.

If Cathy is in the middle of something when the day ends, she files it appropriately.

There's one final technique for maintaining an organized workspace, and that's to add notes where they belong, not on random pieces of paper.

For instance, suppose a client calls Cathy and wants to update her contact information. Instead of jotting it down on a sticky note, Cathy takes out the client's file and adds the information where it belongs.

This technique can save you countless minutes in the run of a day. Think about it – if you jot notes on random pieces of paper, you still have to rewrite the information where it belongs, essentially doubling your work.

It's been mentioned before, but it can't be stressed enough – maintaining an organized workspace is a process, not a one-time event. If you want to optimize your productivity, it's essential that you regularly work at maintaining order.

Question

Addison has been working hard to maintain her organized workspace. She handles each item only once and keeps her filing system up to date.

What are other examples of ways Addison can maintain a productive workspace?

Options:

1. She puts away all her projects at the end of the day, even if she's in the middle of something important

2. She creates a file in her desk drawer where she places all projects she's working on at the end of the day

3. She records all information taken from phone messages in the appropriate files

4. She immediately adds new supplier information to the company's file

5. She tidies her desk at the end of each day, stacking papers in neat piles

6. She creates a file for all the miscellaneous notes she uses to jot down information she will need later

Answer

Option 1: This option is correct. If you want to maintain an organized workspace, you should form a habit of clearing your desk every night. A clean desk can seem like a clean slate, and greeting a new day with a tidy workspace can improve your productivity.

Option 2: This option is correct. To maintain an organized workspace, you should form a habit of clearing your desk every night.

Option 3: This option is correct. You can save time by adding notes where they belong, not on random pieces of paper.

Option 4: This option is correct. To maintain an organized workspace, add notes where they belong, not on random pieces of paper that can be misplaced.

Option 5: This option is incorrect. Actually, one of the keys to an organized workspace is to clear your desk at the end of each day.

Option 6: This option is incorrect. To maintain an organized workspace, you should add notes where they belong, not on random pieces of paper.

CHAPTER 2 - Self-organization and Overcoming Procrastination

Section 1 - Benefits of Overcoming Procrastination

Recognizing workplace procrastination

Recognizing workplace procrastination

Do you ever put off doing tasks that really require your immediate attention? Do you find yourself avoiding tasks rather than tackling them? If you do, you're not alone. This bad habit is commonly called procrastination.

Procrastination occurs in most workplaces. Take the example of Alec, a financial analyst for an insurance company. He must fact-check the organization's financial results before they're published in two days' time.

Alec knows this task will take most of today and tomorrow to complete. However, he convinces himself it's best to wait until tomorrow morning to start, when he's refreshed. So he relaxes by going for coffee with a coworker instead.

This is an example of "tomorrow thinking," where people decide the next day is a better time to handle the task at hand. Instead of working, people distract themselves with less-important activities.

Now consider Cynthia, a sales representative with a data center organization. She's meeting a potential client in two hours and has to prepare a presentation on the virtual data center model. Meanwhile, her colleague must research the client's business history.

However, Cynthia convinces herself she should also research the client's background. Due to her extra research, she runs out of time to complete her presentation and ends up delivering a rushed talk with rough handouts.

Cynthia's behavior is an example of "contingency tomorrow thinking." She throws in extra responsibilities to complicate matters in order to avoid the work originally assigned to her.

Question

Categorize each example of procrastination. More than one example will match each type.

Options:

A. Meena is asked to have her editorial plan finished by close of business but thinks it can wait until tomorrow

B. Ernie's plan today includes an urgent inventory of building supplies, but after a long lunch he pushes this back to tomorrow

C. Jeff has to complete an employee assessment but puts it aside to research assessment methods

D. Derren's marketing report deadline is today but he arranges an unrelated meeting for the afternoon, leaving no time to finish the report

Targets:

1. Contingency tomorrow thinking

2. Tomorrow thinking
Answer

Jeff's decision to research different assessment methodologies before completing his employee assessment review is an example of "contingency tomorrow thinking." Derren's deadline for his marketing report is today, yet instead of addressing that he arranges an unrelated meeting. This is also representative of "contingency tomorrow thinking."

Meena's decision to wait until tomorrow is an example of "tomorrow thinking." Ernie's choice of taking a long lunch and pushing back the inventory is also an example of someone doing tomorrow what should be done today.

The most obvious consequence of procrastination is that a project or task may not be completed on time. However, there are other consequences too. These include stress, anxiety caused by guilt, loss of personal productivity, your colleagues being frustrated, and your organization suffering.

Stress

Procrastination sees unfinished tasks piling up, causing many procrastinators to experience stress. Ignoring work only adds more stress.

Anxiety caused by guilt

As procrastinators feel guilty about incomplete tasks, it leads to an anxiety-led lack of focus and concentration.

Loss of personal productivity

Letting work pile up through procrastination makes it difficult to maintain healthy productivity levels.

Colleagues being frustrated

Procrastinating over a project or task can hold up the work of colleagues relying on its delivery, which can cause frustration.

Your organization suffering

Procrastination has a cumulative effect throughout the organization. It can cost organizations millions of dollars each year.

Question

Remember Cynthia, who ran out of time to create a professional presentation? Cynthia's decision to concentrate on other, less-important matters cost the company a lucrative contract.

What other consequences could Cynthia's procrastinating behavior cause?

Options:

1. The organization may review its approach to such presentations

2. Cynthia might convince herself that her methods weren't flawed

3. The organization might lose millions of dollars due to the lost business

4. Cynthia could feel stressed by her failure to win the company the contract

5. Cynthia may find it hard to concentrate on her next assignment, as she's afraid she'll make the same mistakes

Answer

Option 1: This option is incorrect. It was Cynthia's behavior that was the problem rather than the approach to the presentation.

Option 2: This option is incorrect. Cynthia's failure to win the contract should be indication enough that she wasn't doing the right thing when procrastinating.

Personal Productivity Improvement

Option 3: This option is correct. Cynthia's decision was key to losing the contract, which was potentially worth millions of dollars to the organization.

Option 4: This option is correct. Procrastination can lead to stress, both during the time Cynthia is procrastinating and in the aftermath.

Option 5: This option is correct. This is an example of how procrastination can affect personal productivity.

Causes of workplace procrastination

Causes of workplace procrastination

There are several causes of procrastination. Fear of failing is one cause. Others include fear of giving up control, lack of interest in the task at hand, as well as a feeling of being overwhelmed.

The first common cause of procrastination is fear of failing. If you're faced with a difficult or unfamiliar task you don't feel likely to succeed at, this can lead to procrastination.

Fear of failing can often be the result of placing unrealistic expectations upon yourself.

Take the example of Arnold, a member of a publishing company's Sales Department. His senior vice president asks him to research and assess national buying patterns for e-books and downloaded audiobooks. Arnold has little research experience and is afraid of failing. He avoids getting started on the project for as long as possible, eventually creating a rushed paper that disappoints his superiors.

A second cause of procrastination is fear of giving up control. Procrastinators don't respond well to deadlines, feeling they cause them to lose control of their workflow. Take the example of Cliff, a financial planner with an investment firm's Legal Department. He's writing a department budget plan, which is to be debated before becoming part of the organization's overall budget. Cliff procrastinates so that his proposal won't be ready until after the debate, so it won't be challenged.

Question

Match the actions with the common cause of procrastination they represent. More than one action can match to each cause.

Options:

A. Miles avoids beginning a new web design task, as he's never worked with similar specifications before

B. Larry gives his work to his editor at the last minute to avoid major edits

C. Sharon worries that she can't meet the self-imposed sales target she set for this business quarter and starts avoiding sales calls

D. Hank is late for vital meetings so there isn't enough time to discuss his work

Targets:

1. Fear of failing
2. Fear of giving up control

Answer

Miles's avoidance of his design task happens due to fear of failing at a new, unfamiliar task. Sharon's worry that she won't meet her targets is a result of unrealistic expectations. She procrastinates by abandoning her duties altogether.

Larry's decision to delay handing in his work increases the chances that he stays in control of what's published. Hank's lateness for vital meetings is rooted in not wanting to be judged on his work, and in turn give up control of its contents.

The third common cause of procrastination is a lack of interest in the task at hand. Sometimes you simply want to avoid a boring task that you've been assigned.

Take the example of Elaine, an employee in a financial company's HR Department. Elaine has been asked to reorganize five years of employee complaint files, categorizing them by the manner of complaint.

This task is vital for major changes in the company's employment strategy. However, Elaine feels the task is beneath her and avoids it. As a result, the task isn't completed in time for the employment strategy launch.

The fourth common cause of procrastination is being overwhelmed. This feeling usually manifests itself as an inability to know where to begin a task. Take the example of Silvia, a PR executive with a telecommunications organization. She's controlling the promotion of a nationwide competition for the organization's customer base. Having never organized anything that involved so many different tasks, she avoids beginning the project, delaying it enormously.

Question

Which of these work situations may commonly cause workplace procrastination?

Options:

Personal Productivity Improvement

1. Jenny senses that if the deadline for her production errors report can be delayed she can improve its contents

2. Maxwell feels that unless he delays the delivery of his customer service action plan to his colleagues, it will be completely changed by the time his CEO reads it

3. Liza gets the sense that her organization wants her to delay the delivery of her finance report

4. Bart has never carried out employee assessments before and doesn't know what the first step should be

5. Jenson doesn't think it matters when he starts his IT systems review, as he won't succeed at the task

6. Reena finds the process of filing client documents into specific folders boring

Answer

Option 1: This option is incorrect. This feeling of Jenny's is more of a genuine concern than procrastination.

Option 2: This option is correct. Maxwell procrastinates because he thinks that if he hands over control of his action plan, it may be tampered with.

Option 3: This option is incorrect. While this feeling may cause Liza to procrastinate, this is unlikely to actually happen.

Option 4: This option is correct. Bart is feeling overwhelmed by his task, which can lead to procrastination.

Option 5: This option is correct. Jenson's actions are associated with a fear of failing. This fear can lead to avoiding the task altogether.

Option 6: This option is correct. As Reena doesn't have an interest in her task, she may try to avoid it for as long as she can.

Benefits to overcoming procrastination

Benefits to overcoming procrastination

Imagine what you could accomplish if you were given six more working weeks a year. This is the amount of time most workers waste annually by being disorganized. Remember Alec? He's a financial analyst for an insurance company and a serial procrastinator. As superiors ask him to improve his performance, he could reap many benefits by overcoming his procrastination.

Alec is assigned the task of assessing investment opportunities for the organization. He creates a timetable for completing this task. He adheres to this plan and avoids getting distracted, and for once he delivers a project on time.

Alec's decision to focus on his plan underlines how overcoming procrastination helps you achieve more.

Some estimates say that each minute spent planning results in 10 minutes saved in execution. This equates to a

Personal Productivity Improvement

1,000% return on the time invested. Previously Alec, like many procrastinators, may have claimed he didn't have time to plan. However, the only way this time is ever created is through planning.

Alec observes that to do well professionally, he needs to get organized. He devotes two working days to sorting e-mails into specific folders and organizing physical files that clutter his desk. Over the next two weeks, day-to-day tasks are completed quicker and, with extra time on his hands, the quality of Alec's work improves.

Professional success follows for Alec after his decision to get organized. This shows how Alec, and indeed you, can do better professionally by overcoming procrastination.

Successful people are organized people who avoid procrastination.

Question

Disorganization is harmless and a sign of a creative mind that should be nurtured.

Is the statement true or false?

Options:
1. True
2. False

Answer

Option 1: This statement is not true. Actually, this statement is misleading because disorganization isn't harmless. It can result in lost time and inefficiency.

Option 2: This statement is false. It's misleading because being organized is something that can be learned whether someone has a creative mind or otherwise.

Alec caused a department-wide emergency because his constant procrastination caused a delay in delivery of the organization's financial results. By overcoming procrastination, and planning his workload properly, he can avoid such crises in the future.

Within a few months, Alec becomes better organized and eliminates procrastination, and his stress levels drop significantly. Having previously spent weekends worrying about looming deadlines, he's now free to take that time for himself.

Working in a frantic, unorganized manner, as Alec once did, leads to stress and pressure. Should you overcome procrastination, you'll find you have more time for yourself and to relax too.

Question

Darren is production manager for a global kitchen furniture manufacturer. Recently he's been responsible for several delays in production. He's failed to deliver two vital reports, delayed ordering parts for assembly line machines, and avoided doing two production audits, as he finds auditing bores him.

How would Darren benefit from overcoming procrastination?

Options:

1. He can divide his responsibilities up into the ones he wants to do and the ones he doesn't

2. He could find that he has more time to devote to his life outside the organization, as he's not stressed over missed deadlines

3. He can approach production difficulties in a more professional manner and tackle them right away

4. He's more likely to avoid being the cause of production difficulties

5. He'll find that the production audits are more interesting than he first thought

Personal Productivity Improvement

6. He may find that he achieves more production targets and becomes more at ease with his responsibilities

Answer

Option 1: This option is incorrect. Overcoming procrastination is about facing up to all his responsibilities rather than finding new ways to avoid them.

Option 2: This option is correct. By overcoming procrastination, Darren can forget about work when he goes home.

Option 3: This option is correct. If Darren overcomes procrastination, he can do better professionally. He'll become more adept at completing tasks on time.

Option 4: This option is correct. By overcoming procrastination, Darren can avoid crises that may previously have been common occurrences.

Option 5: This option is incorrect. While this may happen, there's no guarantee of it. However, he will approach the audit in a more professional manner.

Option 6: This option is correct. Overcoming procrastination can lead to Darren achieving more in his workday than previously.

Section 2 - Developing Discipline

Self-discipline

Self-discipline

Have you ever worked diligently on a project to complete it long after your initial enthusiasm has faded? That kind of focus takes self-discipline. This involves both self-knowledge and conscious awareness. It's acting on what you think, rather than what you feel.

Self-discipline is a quality that's generally missing from procrastinators.

While a procrastinator may claim that failure is the result of mismatched skills and tasks, the real cause is often just a lack of self-discipline.

Luckily, self-discipline can be learned. You can develop it into a powerful element of your character.

You may have noted various ways that you could improve your self-discipline. There are four methods. First, you should work during your best times. Second, stop thinking, and just get started. It's also beneficial to make neatness a habit. And finally, focus on finishing.

Developing self-discipline

Developing self-discipline

The first method for becoming self-disciplined is to work during your best times. No one has the same levels of energy and productivity all day. Identify the times you're at your most productive.

To find out when your best times are, chart your energy levels during the course of a day's work. Divide your day into two-hour segments. In each segment, mark down whether your energy levels are high, moderate, or low.

Repeat this across the week to gain an accurate view of your typical working day. Then schedule your most important work for your best hours, when your energy levels are high.

For instance, Morena is an IT consultant who's prone to procrastination. She analyzes her energy levels and finds that she actually works best between 11:00 am and

1:00 pm, so she focuses on her most demanding tasks during that time.

The second method of becoming self-disciplined is to stop thinking and just get started. While preparing your work schedule is important, don't get caught up in planning.

You may have a list of steps drawn up, but if you don't get started, none of the work you've planned will get done. The dread of the work ahead is usually worse than the task itself.

When asked to manage a network infrastructure changeover process for a client, Morena finds the volume of work intimidating. She only gets over this after she begins the project and realizes she can do it.

Question

Match employee actions with the methods for becoming self-disciplined. Both methods may have more than one match.

Options:

A. Jacob realigns his work schedule to reserve his most difficult work for the afternoon, when he's most alert

B. Edith immediately gets to work on research assigned to her by her superiors

C. Jackson realizes that he's losing valuable time worrying about his project and takes corrective action

D. Stephanie divides her workday into sections and measures how motivated she is every 90 minutes

Targets:

1. Stop thinking and just get started
2. Work during your best times

Answer

Personal Productivity Improvement

Edith immediately getting to work on her project and Jackson's realization that he's wasting too much time worrying about his project are examples where people stop thinking and just get started.

Jacob realigning his work schedule to suit his workload and Stephanie dividing her workday into sections are examples of people trying to work during their best times.

The third method for becoming self-disciplined is to make neatness a habit. Neatness helps increase your productivity dramatically. Invest in it and you'll soon save time by not having to sift through clutter. It's not the case that some people are capable of being neat and some aren't. It's a habit that can be learned.

Your ability to find any file you require on an overcrowded computer desktop does not make you disciplined.

If you ask a colleague to find something on your desk or desktop, they should be able to do so easily. You can achieve this by keeping your desk and your computer tidy and clean, and by returning files to their proper places.

Create and maintain digital and paper filing systems if you haven't already done so.

The fourth method that will help you gain self-discipline is to focus on finishing. Work at a steady pace and keep this up.

Try to develop a compulsion for closure as you keep this tempo; focus on finishing rather than getting tied down by perfectionism. Looking for perfectionism isn't a bad trait. However, some people find it hard to let go of a task even when they can't see anything wrong with it.

Don't get sidetracked by something new either. Focus on the task at hand before beginning another.

Punctuating your hard work with rewards helps keep your mind focused on finishing. For example, if you've focused on a task and completed it in three hours, take a small break.

Consider Vincent, an acquisitions manager for a software organization. He's been asked to write a report on a storage services company that may be a new acquisition. He focuses on finishing the report and begins to work at a steady tempo, checking off several key goals early on.

Despite being asked by a colleague to assess another company for acquisition, he concentrates on his own task. Vincent gives himself a five-minute break every time he hits one of the targets involved in finishing the report.

Question

Eliza is a purchasing agent for a mail, package, and freight delivery organization. Her job influences the entire organization's budget. However, Eliza is prone to purchasing materials at the last minute and taking family calls during work time. She's disorganized in filing information on the company's purchases. She also complains that she's never allowed time to work in the mornings when she feels she's at her best. She acknowledges that procrastination is her key problem.

What actions can Eliza take to develop self-discipline in her work?

Options:

1. The next time she gets a project she should try working at a steady tempo and keeping this tempo up

2. She can create a filing system for all purchasing documents on her computer

3. She can decide not to contribute to the budgeting process to make time for newer tasks

4. She can model her workday on that of one of her colleagues

5. She can chart her energy levels during the week to see if the morning really is her most productive time

6. She can stop putting off her work and simply get on with purchasing duties as they're given to her

Answer

Option 1: This option is correct. This is an example of Eliza focusing on finishing. By working at a steady tempo, she can move toward her final goal quicker.

Option 2: This option is correct. This shows Eliza trying to make neatness a habit.

Option 3: This option is incorrect. Instead of facing up to problems, Eliza is passing them on.

Option 4: This option is incorrect. Different people are productive at different times of the day. Eliza must determine her own productive hours.

Option 5: This option is correct. Eliza should reserve the most difficult aspects of her job for her best times and can use the chart to find out when this is.

Option 6: This option is correct. Eliza's decision not to avoid work is indicative of someone who's decided to stop thinking and just get started.

Recognizing and combating time wasters

Recognizing and combating time wasters

You're in the middle of a big project and you need to get back to work, but how about quickly checking your e-mail first? Or perhaps a quick look at your social networking site to see how everyone is? Many people get caught up in these time-wasting activities when they should be working.

Avoiding such time wasters is vital to developing self-discipline. The time and energy wasted isn't confined to the minutes you're on the phone or the Internet. Shifting your attention from your task actually sets you back further in your work, as you need to review what you've done before, wasting more time. Common time wasters are e-mail and the Internet, telephone calls, interruptions from colleagues, personal reading material, and unnecessary meetings.

Combating excessive use of e-mail and Internet browsing takes organization and discipline. Set up separate e-mail accounts for work and personal purposes. Also, stop continuously checking your e-mail; you should do so only at regular intervals. Use e-mail folders and file each message in the appropriate section. As for the Web, think of a task you could be doing instead of surfing and close the browser.

To combat the second common time waster – telephone calls – be disciplined. Family and friends should be told to contact you only in emergencies. Use a similar approach when you're concentrating on an important work task. Let fellow employees know you're only available over the phone if it's regarding an urgent matter.

The third common time waster is interruptions from colleagues. The best way to combat this is to inform colleagues when you're available to talk. If necessary, find a new space to work in. Be it at home or elsewhere in your office, this frees you from interruption. If you have an office with a door, you can close it to minimize disruption. Also, organizations can create a designated quiet time where employees work without interruption.

Question

What are methods of combating time wasters?

Options:

1. Alternate between days when you can take personal calls and days you take business calls

2. Close the door to your office for long periods of the day

3. Inspect all links contained in e-mails to see if they're of benefit to you

4. Tell family and friends you can't be reached by phone during work hours unless there is an emergency

5. Set up a separate e-mail account for your personal e-mails from friends

Answer

Option 1: This option is incorrect. Personal calls should really only happen in emergencies.

Option 2: This option is correct. This action signifies that you want to be left alone, thus limiting interruptions from colleagues.

Option 3: This option is incorrect. This action can lead to excessive web browsing as you check each and every link.

Option 4: This option is correct. By telling your family and friends not to call you during work hours, you're eliminating distracting phone calls from your day.

Option 5: This option is correct. By separating personal e-mails into another account, you won't be distracted by private matters during work hours.

Personal reading material is the fourth common time waster that must be combated.

Clear your work space of reading material, such as newspapers or magazines that don't concern your work.

The fifth and final time waster is unnecessary meetings. Be sure the meetings you do attend have a clear agenda. Don't let meetings run longer than scheduled, and make sure you assign action items.

Employees consistently encounter these time wasters and must learn to combat them. For example, Barry, who's a researcher with an IT security services provider, has received complaints regarding the pace of his work.

Personal Productivity Improvement

He realizes that he often spends up to an hour a day checking his e-mail. He combats this by deciding on a limit of checking his e-mail once every 90 minutes.

Barry was also recently in the middle of researching competing products when his brother called. When Barry returned to his work, it took him 20 minutes to refocus on the project. Barry asks his family and friends to only contact him during work hours in emergencies.

Recently, when preparing a document on web security, Barry was held up by colleagues asking his opinion on security issues. To prevent a repeat of this, Barry suggests to HR that the company designate "quiet times" for each department.

Whenever he's stressed with work, Barry admits that he often relaxes by reading a sports magazine he subscribes to. After realizing how much time he actually spends doing it, he resolves to clear his desk of all non-work-related reading material.

Finally, Barry meets with his superiors to discuss why he's spending 45% of his time in meetings. Only the product development meetings concern his workload, so he gets agreement that he can skip attending other meetings. Barry finds he gets a lot more done since eliminating this range of time- wasting activities.

Question

Match the actions with the time wasters they're attempting to combat.

Options:

A. Julio creates two separate inboxes that filter work and private messages

B. Xavier often works at home during the afternoons

C. George only talks to friends over the phone outside of work hours

D. Ellen stops printing non-work-related news articles for quieter work hours

E. Tanya creates an agenda for her meeting with the HR Department

Targets:
1. Telephone calls
2. E-mail and browsing the Internet
3. Time-wasting meetings
4. Reading material
5. Interruptions from colleagues

Answer

George's decision to only talk to his friends outside of work hours indicates he doesn't want them to call and distract him from his duties.

Julio's decision to create two inboxes for work and personal e-mails is a way of tackling excessive e-mail checking and Internet browsing.

Tanya's idea to create a clear agenda for a meeting with her HR personnel indicates she's making sure it's not a meeting where time is wasted.

Ellen's decision to stop printing non-work-related articles means she's aware that devoting time to such reading material during work hours can be wasteful.

Xavier's decision to work at home will help decrease interruptions from colleagues. He can control which colleagues he talks to from home.

You should identify your personal time wasters that impact your workday. Perhaps it's the 15-minute break that turns into a 30-minute one. Or maybe it's the unnecessary and energy-sapping meetings.

Make a list explaining the actions you need to take to stop these time wasters. For instance, if one time waster you've identified is that your lunch break runs long because you eat in front of your computer while reading the news online, add "eat lunch in the cafeteria" to your list.

Then place the list of actions in your office in a prominent position as a reminder not to give in to time wasters.

Case Study: Question 1 of 3
Scenario

Imagine you're a marketing coordinator with a sustainable energy organization. Answer the questions that address time wasters, in order.

Question

What activities in your typical day as a marketing coordinator should you avoid to build self-discipline and avoid procrastination?

Options:

1. Attending meetings on marketing and product development matters

2. Reading fashion magazines

3. Taking calls from friends and colleagues that aren't work related

4. Chatting with colleagues who drop by your office

5. Reading up on sustainable energy

6. Getting distracted by non-related links when carrying out research

Answer

Option 1: This option is incorrect. These meetings are important from the perspective of a marketing coordinator.

Option 2: This option is correct. Reading this non-work-related material is wasting time and should be done on your own time.

Option 3: This option is correct. Telephone calls from colleagues and friends won't always be related to work.

Option 4: This option is correct. Interruptions from colleagues break the flow of your day and make it difficult to keep your mind on your work. You should be direct in how you want to use your work time.

Option 5: This option is incorrect. As the company's marketing coordinator, you need to be up to date on sustainable energy.

Option 6: This option is correct. Excessive Internet usage can only be avoided by discipline.

Case Study: Question 2 of 3

How could you combat the time wasters identified in your normal day as a marketing coordinator?

Options:

1. Remove yourself from all situations where you have to talk to colleagues

2. Remove fashion magazines from your work area

3. Ask colleagues and friends to call you only when absolutely necessary

4. Identify hours of the working day where friends and family can call you

5. Inform colleagues when you're available to talk face-to-face

6. Close your Internet browser if you find yourself on non-work-related sites

Answer

Option 1: This option is incorrect. There are important meetings you must attend, and these will involve colleagues.

Option 2: This option is correct. If non-work-related reading material is removed from your office, it can't distract you.

Option 3: This option is correct. This will save you from time-wasting interruptions.

Option 4: This option is incorrect. You should tell friends and family to only call you during work hours in emergencies.

Option 5: This option is correct. You should inform colleagues when you can't talk to them and when you can.

Option 6: This option is correct. The Internet is one of the greatest time wasters and it's essential to focus on using it to achieve work goals.

Case Study: Question 3 of 3

You've been asked to attend a meeting on sustainable energy sales strategies by your company.

What actions should you take to make sure this meeting isn't a time waster for you?

Options:

1. Make sure to bring along suggestions for sales strategies

2. Make sure the content actually relates directly to your marketing function

3. Set aside a specific amount of time for the meeting and stick to it

4. Ensure the meeting has a defined end time and that you have specific action items from the meeting

Answer

Option 1: This option is incorrect. Only do this if asked to do so, as carrying out this task may waste time.

Option 2: This option is correct. Time-wasting meetings are usually ones filled with content unrelated to your work.

Option 3: This option is incorrect. This could be counterproductive, as you may end up wasting time trying to find out what happened after you leave.

Option 4: This option is correct. By making sure the meeting has a structure, you can be assured that its content is valuable.

Section 3 - Setting Your Priorities

Setting priorities and keeping focused

Setting priorities and keeping focused

Setting priorities is key to an effective and directed life. A lot of people say that their priority in life is their family. Setting priorities, and accepting responsibility for those priorities, is important in the workplace too. Focus on achieving them rather than the reasons they're difficult to achieve.

Decide on set priorities and stay focused on them. Four actions are key to keeping focused: clearly define your goals, prioritize your activities, break projects into elements, and become a planner.

The first action to take in order to set priorities and keep focused is to clearly define your goals. Staying on track during any workplace project requires having direction, and this is what your goals provide.

Make your goals measurable and specific in order to keep track of their success.

When focusing on your goals, filter out outside distractions. Try not to get distracted by other concerns or colleague interruptions.

Goals have two purposes. The first is to narrow the range of options available to distract you. The second purpose of a goal is to make you concentrate on your destination.

For instance, Zane is a production manager with a home furnishings organization. At the beginning of each month he sets out his goals. This month, they include production meetings, equipment purchasing, equipment research, and performance audits. He maps out a schedule of these tasks and specifically marks them as "done" once he completes them.

Question

Which actions help in reaching your defined goals?

Options:

1. Setting goals that are attainable within a short period of time

2. Avoiding any distractions that take attention away from your goals

3. Translating your targets into measurable parts

4. Creating goals that are within your skill set

Answer

Option 1: This option is incorrect. You can't always ensure that goals can be reached in a short amount of time.

Option 2: This option is correct. By avoiding distraction, you can concentrate fully on achieving the goals you've set for yourself.

Option 3: This option is correct. By breaking down your goals into measurable parts, you can keep track of whether or not you're going in the right direction.

Option 4: This option is incorrect. Your goals may involve attaining new skills or learning new techniques along the way.

The second way of ensuring you keep focused on your goals is to prioritize your activities.

It's important to take an overview of your work activities and work out which ones to prioritize. Often, it's best to arrange them into three sections.

As you begin setting priorities, the first of the three sections includes low-priority activities, which can be

delegated to others or completed when you have time. The second section should include medium- priority activities that must have attention paid to them, although they can be set aside for more

important tasks if any arise. The final section includes high-priority activities. These are important to you and your organization and must be completed urgently.

Don't overreach and take on added responsibilities if they're not essential. Tasks you've marked as low- priority activities can possibly be dealt with without your participation. You could delegate these tasks to

colleagues who can spare the time, or bring someone in specifically for these activities. Make sure delegation is worthwhile to you and the person you've delegated to.

Take the example of Mildred, a public relations executive with an electronics manufacturer. Mildred's approach to work is to take on each task when she thinks of it. This leads to a lack of contribution to some important ad campaigns due to time-consuming tasks like follow-up e-mails to journalists.

Determined to prioritize her activities effectively, Mildred lists her tasks for the week ahead. She has to work with the Product Development Department on a marketing strategy for a new product, arrange radio interviews involving the organization's CEO, and meet with a TV advertising agency regarding a new campaign.

She begins to sort these activities. Her work with the Product Development Department is high priority, as the new product is important to the company. Meeting with the TV advertising agency is of medium priority, as the campaign is still some months away. The radio interviews are classed as low priority, so Mildred asks a colleague in need of experience to arrange them instead.

Question

Match the employee actions with the methods of keeping focused and setting priorities. Each method may have more than one match.

Options:

A. John divides his quarterly sales target into quantifiable elements

B. Cliff's time will be better spent assessing sales figures, so he delegates performance audits to Mark

C. Zara concentrates on getting her employee audits done and avoids distractions

D. Denise divides her responsibilities into three sections depending on importance

Targets:

1. Clearly define your goals
2. Prioritize your activities

Answer

John's decision to divide up his sales target into measurable parts and Zara's determination to avoid distractions are examples of clearly defining your goals.

Cliff's acknowledgment that his time is better spent on something else and that he should delegate other duties to Mark shows he's able to prioritize his activities. Denise's decision to divide her responsibilities in order of importance allows her to prioritize tasks.

Breaking things down and planning

Breaking things down and planning

The third way of setting your priorities and ensuring you keep focused on your goals is to break projects into elements that can be completed one at a time.

Take the example of Dale, a financial director with a health food producer. He has to complete the organization's budget before the end of the year. The task is so large that it's seen as a one-month process, and Dale starts by breaking the task into achievable elements.

This includes first meeting with all department managers and then assessing each department's budgetary needs. Dale also has to research the financial impact of any interest rate increases and food legislation changes. He has to write up the budget, run it by his CEO, and make changes where necessary.

Dale keeps tabs on all these elements, crossing off each one as it is achieved.

The fourth recommended action to help set priorities and keep focused is to become a planner. Planning is a skill that can be learned. When working toward a goal, the more complete a plan is, the better its chance of success.

For every one minute you spend planning, it's estimated ten minutes are saved during execution. If you want to gain that extra time, there are three rules to planning that should be adhered to each day: be a continuous planner, start your day early, and finish your day planning the next.

Be a continuous planner

As you move through a plan, continuously add to it. Analyze your success as you work, and change or alter your plan as necessary.

For example, Erika is an online advertising consultant for a commercial bank. She's working on a major Internet ad campaign for the organization. She adds other targets to her plan as she moves along, including creating an additional mobile application related to the campaign market. She adjusts her plan as necessary to fit this in.

Start your day early

The more time you have, the better, so begin your day early. Reflect on how your goals will be achieved. Then use these reflections to create your action plan for the day.

In Erika's case, when she arrives at work she begins each day early by planning out meetings with the bank's online creative team, public relations division, and mobile applications experts. She also highlights when status reports on the project are due to the CEO.

Finish your day planning

When finishing your workday, begin to plan the next one. List the activities that will need your attention the next day.

Erika ends her day by assessing the impact of her meetings and filing her status report. If any campaign action points are to be completed the next day she highlights them. She sets reminders for tomorrow's meetings as well, mapping out her time so she can complete all her duties.

Question

Jason is a project manager with a global car manufacturer. He's organizing the development process for a new car design but is struggling to keep focused.

How can Jason help himself set priorities and keep focused?

Options:

1. Jason needs to review whether or not the development process is necessary

2. Jason can ask his colleagues to prioritize his tasks

3. Jason should list all his tasks in the development process and categorize each by low, medium, or high importance

4. Jason can establish a list of the key outcomes this process must achieve

5. Jason needs to begin each working day by setting out what exactly he has to achieve by the close of business

6. Jason can split the development process into sections such as meetings, deadlines, and delivery processes

Answer

Option 1: This option is incorrect. This is a way of avoiding his duties. Jason should get started on setting his priorities instead.

Option 2: This option is incorrect. This sees Jason relying on others to set his priorities rather than himself.

Option 3: This option is correct. By prioritizing his activities in order, Jason ensures he's focusing the requisite amount of energy on each activity.

Option 4: This option is correct. By setting out the eventual goals of the process, Jason can focus on them.

Option 5: This option is correct. This is what Jason should do if he's going to become a planner. Such a move would be of great benefit to ensuring he stays focused on what exactly he needs to achieve.

Option 6: This option is correct. This is an example of Jason breaking projects into elements that can be measured and accounted for while being achieved one at a time.

Steps to help you say "no"

Steps to help you say "no"

Many people are prone to becoming overcommitted. Unable to say "no" to any task they're asked to do leads to inflated workloads. Sound familiar? Feeling overwhelmed, many people will procrastinate in this situation and avoid starting that large workload altogether.

Many workers will assume they can't say "no" when asked to perform a task. However, learning to say "no", and meaning it, is a big part of setting your priorities.

The displeasure you'll encounter from saying "no" is nothing compared to the displeasure encountered by failing to deliver.

To help you say "no" when necessary, be clear about your priorities and stick to them. Avoid getting sidetracked by new assignments or distractions. Say "no" to anything that diverts you away from achieving your goals.

Question

Think about your own work situation. How over-commited are you in your job?

Options:
1. Very over-commited
2. Somewhat over-commited
3. Not over-commited

Answer

Option 1: You say you're very over-commited. This could be due to you assuming you can't say "no" to tasks. Consider the methods that follow for combating overcommitment and saying "no."

Option 2: You say you're somewhat over-commited. It's likely you need help with developing your ability to say "no." You can build on this ability by reviewing the steps that follow.

Option 3: You say you're not over-committed. This indicates that you know when to say "no" to a new task. You can build on this ability by reviewing the steps that follow.

There are four steps that can be helpful in developing an ability to say "no" and avoiding overcommitment. First give yourself permission to say "no." Second, explain that you need to be realistic about the consequences of the commitment. Third, be direct and assertive, and fourth, offer alternatives and solutions.

A first step many will find helpful in saying "no" to overcommitment is giving yourself permission to say "no." You have to learn to value your own time.

Don't feel guilty for not giving your time up. People often feel guilty about letting someone, or an organization, down by saying "no." To help ward off this guilt, remind yourself why you're saying "no."

For example, Keith, a distribution channel manager with a GPS manufacturer, is feeling guilty for not taking on a new project. His department director asked him to create a financial action plan. Keith now finds it hard to concentrate on his normal work due to the guilt he feels for turning the task down. He only gets over this by reminding himself how important the time spent on his current tasks is.

The second step that can be helpful in saying "no" to overcommitment is to be realistic about the consequences of any commitment.

Study the commitments you've already made to be sure you can take on something else.

Don't feel you have to answer on the spot. If necessary, tell the person handing you the task you'll get back to her later.

Take the example of Estelle, a marketing employee with a clothing organization. She's asked by her manager, Tom, to interview all 130 international sales employees to get product feedback.

The task must be complete within 3 weeks, and each interview has a set format of 10 minutes. Estelle tells Tom she'll have to review her schedule and get back to him.

Her monthly workload list shows she has space for 3 hours a week to work on the project. However, across the 3 weeks this would only allow her to interview 54 sales employees. Estelle then says "no" to the project.

Question

Which statements represent effective ways of saying "no?"

Options:
1. "I didn't feel guilty about turning down the design project because I didn't like the work involved."
2. "My time is valuable and my expertise is needed more urgently on other projects."
3. "I don't have much time to get it done, but doing this research project will get me a promotion."
4. "I have only three hours free next week and your project requires a day-long commitment."

Answer

Option 1: This option is incorrect. Turning down work because you don't like it isn't a valid reason for saying "no."

Option 2: This option is correct. Not feeling guilty about turning down a project or task is part of giving yourself permission to say "no" and recognizing that your time is important.

Option 3: This option is incorrect. You can't pick and choose tasks based on promotion prospects.

Option 4: This option is correct. This is part of being realistic about the consequences of taking on extra work.

A third helpful step in saying "no" to overcommitment is to be direct and assertive. Be firm but polite – don't be too nice when saying "no," but don't be rude either. It's also often a good idea to communicate the reasons for saying no, such as an upcoming deadline that you are already committed to.

Remember Keith the channel manager? His department director has asked him to explain why he didn't take on the financial action plan. Keith makes a list of the reasons he can't undertake it, including his expertise level and a worry that his lack of experience would lead to another employee revising his attempted plan. He relays these reasons calmly to his department director, who approves of his actions.

The fourth step in saying "no" to overcommitment is to offer alternatives and solutions. One method is to propose changing work priorities. If your manager asks you to do something, you work out a way where current priorities are given less time, delayed, or even dropped.

You could also think about switching around tasks. Replacing planned tasks with the one you've said "no" to may be feasible. A final solution is redelegating. Discuss whether some work can be redelegated to allow you to take on something new.

Also think about deferring – if you need more time to weigh up the task, ask for it. This time must be used to genuinely consider the implications of committing to the task, rather than merely procrastinating.

Keith is asked by his department director to contribute to a training program for production managers. Keith doesn't feel he has the time, and asks if he can prioritize the program over warehouse inspections. When turned down, he suggests switching responsibility over to another channel manager. This is also refused, so Keith defers his decision. He then suggests delegating half the training program responsibilities to a fellow channel manager. With Keith managing the other half of the project, this proposal is accepted.

Case Study: Question 1 of 2
Scenario

Raymond manages the Finance Department of a broadband provider. Access the learning aid

Raymond's Situation to find out the details of the situation.

Answer the questions in order to address how Raymond deals with overcommitment.

Question

What are the first things Raymond should do in order to prove to himself and others that he didn't have the time to take on his CEO's request?

Options:

1. He should take a realistic look at the amount of work he already has on his plate

2. He should work late into the evening every night just to demonstrate how busy he is

3. He should delegate the task immediately

4. He should realize that he can't give up his time to work on projects that will only harm his regular work

Answer

Option 1: This option is correct. This assessment takes into account his current commitments and how they would be disrupted by taking on the new task.

Option 2: This option is incorrect. Working late to demonstrate commitment is not an effective way to reflect his lack of time.

Option 3: This option is incorrect. This is not the first thing Raymond needs to do. First he must give himself permission to say "no" and he must assess his work situation.

Option 4: This option is correct. This action will help Raymond give himself permission to say "no." By realizing his time is valuable, he won't waste it by taking on work that others can do.

Case Study: Question 2 of 2

Despite initially accepting Raymond's decision, his CEO soon comes back to him and says he can't take "no" for an answer.

Which statements show Raymond effectively offering an alternative solution to his boss?

Options:

1. "I'll take on the document, but I'll have to delay employee assessments."
2. "I can take responsibility for the market expansion document if no one else can."
3. "I can attend the brainstorming meetings and may need help with writing the document."
4. "I can take on this project, but I'll have to cancel team meetings for the next four weeks."
5. "I can't take this on at the moment, but if it can wait until next month, I may have some free time."
6. "I can attend the brainstorming meetings, but maybe our HR manager could manage the document instead."

Answer

Option 1: This option is correct. This shows Raymond trying to change priorities by offering to delay other commitments to take on the new one.

Option 2: This option is incorrect. This isn't a constructive solution. Raymond knows he doesn't have the necessary time, and ultimately this will hinder both him and the organization.

Option 3: This option is incorrect. Raymond has to be clear on how he'll take part, or not take part, in the market expansion document. This statement doesn't offer an alternative or a solution.

Option 4: This option is correct. Raymond's decision to switch around tasks by canceling team meetings in favor of the document project is one way of offering an alternative solution to the issue.

Option 5: This option is correct. Deferring his decision on the task is one way of offering an alternative to Raymond's CEO.

Option 6: This option is correct. Raymond can attempt to delegate responsibility for the task to someone else.

CHAPTER 3 - Managing Tasks and Maximizing Productivity

Section 1 - Assessing Your Time and Setting Priorities

The value of setting goals

The value of setting goals

Time treats everybody equally. No matter who you are, where you live, or what job you do, you only have 24 hours a day to get things done. So to make the most of the time you have, you need to learn to focus on what's important – those activities that provide the most value.

Time management is a way to assess and prioritize your time to organize your work processes for maximum efficiency, effectiveness, and productivity.

Successful businesspeople appreciate the value of their time. They realize that time needs to be managed just like any other valuable asset.

These high achievers understand the importance of a clear set of goals. They don't stumble into achievement. They set targets early on and use their time effectively to work toward success.

There are many benefits of setting goals. When you have goals in mind, you'll be better able to define what you want out of your career. You'll be able to establish specific targets to help you advance, and you'll be able to measure your progress toward reaching those targets. Setting goals also provides a framework on which you can build an effective and efficient work schedule.

Define what you want

You'll have a better chance of meeting expectations if you understand how your efforts contribute to achieving your goals. For example, you might define specific goals to work toward. This helps increase your personal efficiency, and ultimately the achievement of both personal and business objectives.

Establish targets

Once you decide what you want to achieve, you'll need to determine how to get there. Setting goals helps you establish targets – measurable steps in the strategic path toward your goals. Setting and achieving targets moves you incrementally toward achieving your long-term goals. For example, a salesperson might establish monthly sales targets.

Measure progress

Setting goals helps you measure your progress. For example, comparing goals with actual results tells you if you're on the right track. This helps you assess and facilitate the flow of work, and ensure that your attention and efforts aren't being wasted.

Provide a framework

Your goals provide you with a framework that allows you to schedule your time effectively. Goals also help you

Personal Productivity Improvement

organize key work activities so they align with your long-term strategic path.

Question

Consider Andre, a research and development manager at a software company. Recently, his workload has increased. In addition to his regular duties, he's currently working on several projects and is also acting as a mentor in the company's succession planning program. Andre needs help managing his time but he's confused about where to start.

How will setting goals be of value to Andre in assessing his time and setting priorities?

Options:

1. It will help him define what he wants out of his job
2. It will help him establish clear targets
3. He'll be able to measure his success
4. It will provide him with a framework for deciding how to spend his time
5. He'll have something to refer to if he starts to fall behind in his work
6. He'll be guaranteed a successful future

Answer

Option 1: This option is correct. The process of setting specific goals will help Andre understand and define what he wants to achieve.

Option 2: This option is correct. Setting goals will help Andre establish the targets he needs to meet to move toward achieving those goals.

Option 3: This option is correct. Setting goals will allow Andre to measure his progress along the path to reaching those targets.

Option 4: This option is correct. Goals are the basis for a framework Andre can use to build an effective and efficient schedule for his time.

Option 5: This option is incorrect. Andre won't be able to organize his time efficiently if he doesn't use his goals as the basis for organizing and prioritizing his time.

Option 6: This option is incorrect. Setting goals can't guarantee success, but Andre is more likely to be successful if he has a clear set of goals and a plan for achieving those goals.

The Pareto principle

The Pareto principle

Time management involves establishing what you need to accomplish – your targets and goals – and then comparing that with what you actually are accomplishing. Your degree of success – or personal productivity – will depend on your ability to set priorities for your tasks and activities.

Question

How much of your average workday would you say is truly productive?

Options:

1. Very little of the day
2. Some of the day
3. Most of the day

Answer

Option 1: You noted that very little of your day is productive. But don't despair. There are principles and strategies that can help you make the most out of the time you have.

Option 2: You noted that some of your day is productive. You're on the right track, but your productivity could likely be improved by learning about how to assess the time you have and set relevant priorities.

Option 3: You noted that most of your day is productive. It's great to have confidence in your ability to produce value, but remember that things can change quickly. The ability to assess your time and set relevant priorities is important to setting a resilient and robust strategic path.

Good productivity isn't just a result of hard work and dedication. If goals and work efforts are not properly aligned, your results will be disappointing.

Improving productivity involves a concerted effort to take control of those things that have a detrimental effect on progress toward achieving your goals.

But sometimes it's difficult to know where to begin. In cases like this it can help to start with one of the better known principles of business – the Pareto principle.

The "Pareto principle"– also known as the 80/20 rule – deals with cause and effect. It asserts that 80% of effects come from 20% of causes. When the best approach to achieving your goal is unclear, applying the Pareto principle can give you a point at which to begin.

Applying the Pareto principle to personal productivity suggests that 20% of the tasks you perform result in 80% of the successful results you achieve. So it makes sense to identify the most valuable tasks in your schedule and devote more time to them.

Question

Personal Productivity Improvement

What are possible applications of the Pareto principle?

Options:

1. 80% of successful results come from 20% of scheduled activities
2. 80% of causes result in 20% of computer errors
3. 80% of a company's sales come from 20% of its customers
4. 80% of mistakes result in 20% of lost time

Answer

Option 1: This option is correct. The Pareto principle deals with cause and effect. In this case, 20% of activities cause 80% of targeted results.

Option 2: This option is incorrect. The basic Pareto principle states that 80% of effects come from 20% of causes.

Option 3: This option is correct. In this case, 20% of the customers cause 80% of sales to happen. Productivity could be increased by concentrating on that 20%.

Option 4: This option is incorrect. The Pareto principle is that 80% of effects come from 20% of causes. This example states the opposite.

Assessing time and prioritizing tasks

Assessing time and prioritizing tasks

If someone asked you how you spend your time in a typical workday, would you be able to do it? You'd likely remember the more important or interesting tasks. And you'd probably remember scheduled events such as meetings. But what about all the other things you do?

It's difficult to accurately gauge how much time you spend doing your job. This is because the mind tends to forget the routine tasks and more mundane activities that make up so much of a typical workday.

To get the most value out of your time, you'll need to get an accurate picture of your workday.

First, you'll need to identify how you spend your time, and then assess whether you're spending that time wisely.

There are four steps to assessing your time and prioritizing your tasks. Step one is to log your time. Step two is to use your log to find patterns of time use. Step three is to analyze your tasks in terms of your goals. And step four is to use the information you've gathered to identify your priorities – those activities that produce the most value.

1. Log your time

Your first step is to log your time by writing down each task you perform, when you perform that task, and the time the task takes to complete.

2. Find patterns

Next, you'll review your task logs and find patterns of time use. This is where you'll identify what you're really spending your time doing.

3. Analyze tasks

Then you'll analyze your tasks. Here you'll check each of your tasks and categories of tasks and consider how well each aligns with your key responsibilities and goals.

4. Identify priorities

Finally, you'll identify your priorities by assessing the importance and urgency of your logged tasks.

Step one of assessing time and prioritizing tasks is logging your time. To get an accurate assessment of how you spend your time, you need to construct a written record – a task log of your workday.

A task log is a written or electronic record used to track the precise amount of time you spend on various tasks each day. Typically, the logging form will have columns where you'll list the task, time started, and minutes used.

These are followed by columns where you'll categorize your tasks. These general activity categories should be tailored to your job or profession.

Be sure to log each task as you do it, and make a log entry every time you change activities. Include personal tasks such as calling home, and distractions such as browsing online. And don't neglect small tasks such as traveling to an internal meeting. Over time, these short periods can add up to a considerable chunk of time.

Step two of assessing time and prioritizing tasks is to find the patterns in your time use. To do this, you'd gather your task logs for one week. Analyzing your work week will provide enough data to identify both how you spend your time, and the times at which you're the most productive.

Since you've categorized your tasks in the logs, it will be easy to analyze imbalances in the types of tasks on which you're spending time. For example, do your logs show you're spending much of your time doing paperwork or talking on the phone?

Or perhaps you're using much of your workday helping or socializing with colleagues at work. Maybe there are times of day when you get a lot of interruptions. Your logs can show you these patterns.

Of course, you'll have to assess your time use patterns in terms of your own job responsibilities. For example, spending most of the day in the office doing paperwork may be appropriate for an accountant, but counterproductive for a sales representative.

Highlighting "time-wasters" in your logs can show you where there's room to improve your productivity. It can also point out areas of fragmentation – for example, times of day when you get a lot of interruptions.

Step three of assessing time and prioritizing tasks is to consider your tasks in terms of both goals and consequences. Remember that your most important tasks and activities are those that produce the most value.

Highest value tasks are those that are both aligned to your goals and have a high potential to impact the success of your work.

Check your logs and consider which of your tasks and activities provide strategic value. Ask yourself, "How does this task contribute toward achieving my goals?" Tasks and activities that move you in the right strategic direction are more important than those that don't.

You should also consider tasks and activities in terms of consequences – the potential impact of the task. Here you should ask yourself, "What are the possible consequences of not doing this task?"

It's important not to ignore assessing the consequences of your tasks. For example, routine or mundane tasks such as checking e-mail may seem to have little strategic value. But if you miss an important message from a client, it could have serious consequences.

Question

Match each strategy to the most appropriate questions you could ask to use that strategy in assessing your time logs. Each strategy may match to more than one question.

Options:

A. Find patterns of time use in your logs
B. Consider tasks in terms of goals and consequences

Targets:

1. Are any particular tasks or activities taking up a lot of my time?
2. Are there any times of day when I get a lot of interruptions?
3. How does this task contribute toward achieving my objectives?
4. What could happen if I didn't do this task?

Answer

Looking for patterns in your time use can help you determine how efficiently your schedule is organized.

Your logs show patterns of time use, such as those periods when your time use is fragmented by a lot of interruptions.

It's important to consider tasks in terms of goals. Your most valuable tasks and activities are those that move you in the right strategic direction.

You can get an idea of a task's value by considering the consequences of completing or not completing each one.

Using a priorities matrix

Using a priorities matrix

Step four of assessing time and prioritizing tasks is to identify your priorities. Priorities are those tasks and activities that take precedence over others.

Question

How do you usually prioritize your tasks?

Options:

1. I start with the routine or easier tasks
2. I do the most urgent tasks first
3. I begin with the more difficult or important tasks

Answer

Option 1: You noted you start with routine or easy tasks. This may seem like a way to reduce the number of things you have to do. However, focusing on the smaller tasks can eat away at your time, leaving more valuable tasks undone.

Option 2: You noted you start with the most urgent tasks. You're not alone. Many people have the tendency to leave tasks until time becomes an issue. But focusing on urgent issues can have a detrimental effect on longer-term, high value tasks that require an investment of your time.

Option 3: You noted you start with the more difficult or important tasks. These are often the tasks that provide the most value, but don't forget about the smaller and time-sensitive tasks. These can have serious consequences if left undone.

Critical

Tasks that are both time-sensitive and high value are critical priorities. This includes crises, deadlines, and business commitments to others. Examples include producing a weekly departmental report for your boss, compiling an agenda for a management meeting tomorrow, or compiling a list of project requirements for a client you're meeting this afternoon.

High

Tasks that are high value, but not time-sensitive, are high priorities. These are tasks that involve thinking, planning, and collaboration. Although these tasks fall into your longer-term plans, they should be started as soon as possible. If you leave them too long, they can become time-sensitive. These tasks include strategic planning, building relationships, and personal development. Examples include booking a location for the annual general meeting, meeting with potential clients, or making sales calls.

Medium

Tasks that are time-sensitive, but not high value, are medium priorities. These are often tasks that can be dealt with quickly, during shorter gaps in your schedule. This includes some meetings, some correspondence, and requests for assistance from colleagues. Examples include responding to general e-mail, proofing a colleague's paperwork, or answering your phone.

Low

Tasks that are neither time-sensitive nor high value are low priority. These are tasks that can be put off to another time, dropped entirely from your schedule, or delegated to someone else. This includes time-wasters, doing favors for others, and some correspondence and meetings. Examples include helping a colleague learn the new computer system, researching a new car on the Internet, or booking your travel for a conference next year.

A priority matrix is useful for prioritizing the activities in your daily task logs. To prioritize your tasks, consider where each task would fit in terms of the matrix. Make a list and write down a priority for each task in your logs. Use 1 for critical tasks – those that are time-sensitive and high value. Use 2 for high – high value but not time-sensitive. Use 3 for medium – time-sensitive, but low value, and use 4 for low – neither time-sensitive nor high value.

Consider Jennifer, an editorial manager at a publishing company. Her long-term goals involve getting books to market on schedule, and acquiring talented new authors.

Jennifer has logged her tasks each day for a week. She's now ready to prioritize her tasks and determine how she's spending her time. She begins with Monday morning.

Jennifer notes much of Monday morning was spent checking the edits on the final manuscript of a novel so she could send it to the printers. She notices a pattern of interruptions during this task – mostly visits from colleagues. She then analyzes her tasks in terms of goals and consequences. This gives her the high value tasks. Jennifer then determines which tasks are time-sensitive. Finally, she uses a priority matrix to assign a priority to each of her tasks. Her highest priority tasks are both high value and time-sensitive.

Jennifer's tasks that are both high value and time-sensitive are categorized as critical priority and rated 1. The tasks that are high value but not time-sensitive are categorized as high priority and rated 2. The tasks that are time-sensitive but low value are categorized as medium priority and rated 3. The tasks that are neither high value nor time-sensitive are categorized as low priority and rated 4.

Question

What are the characteristics of critical tasks on a priority matrix?

Options:

1. High value and time-sensitive
2. High value but not time-sensitive
3. Time-sensitive but low value

Answer

Option 1: This is the correct option. Tasks that are high value and time-sensitive are critical tasks.

Option 2: This option is incorrect. Tasks that are high value but not time-sensitive are high-priority tasks.

Option 3: This option is incorrect. Tasks that are time-sensitive but low value are medium-priority tasks.

Case Study: Question 1 of 2
Scenario

Personal Productivity Improvement

Raj is a sales representative for an office supply company. He has two main long-term goals. One is meeting his monthly, quarterly, and yearly sales targets. The other is increasing his client base. Raj is very busy and he's seeking to optimize the time he has available by assessing and prioritizing his tasks and activities. Raj has been keeping task logs for a week.

Refer to the learning aid Raj's Task Log to review a portion of Raj's task logs. Answer each question in order.

Question

Which of the tasks in Raj's task log are low priority tasks?

Options:

1. Help Alice set up new computer
2. Visit from Mike
3. Meeting with prospective client
4. Submit sales figures to Finance Department

Answer

Option 1: This option is correct. It's not wrong to help colleagues, but this item isn't aligned with Raj's goals and isn't a high priority task.

Option 2: This option is correct. Social contact is pleasurable, but there won't be any consequences to delaying it.

Option 3: This option isn't correct. This is a high value task. Meeting with clients is aligned to Raj's goal of increasing his client base. As well, there would be negative consequences to missing the meeting.

Option 4: This option isn't correct. Submitting sales figures to Finance Department is aligned with Raj's goal of meeting his sales targets.

Case Study: Question 2 of 2

What are critical priorities on Raj's task list?

Options:

1. Set up account for new client
2. Proof sales figures for month end report deadline
3. Phone prospective client
4. Book booth for fall trade show

Answer

Option 1: This option is correct. This is a critical priority because it's both time-sensitive and high value.

Option 2: This option is correct. Critical priorities involve crises, deadlines, and business commitments

to others. This task is also aligned to Raj's goals.

Option 3: This option is incorrect. This is a high priority task, but it isn't critical because it isn't time-sensitive.

Option 4: This option is incorrect. Raj can afford to wait to do this task. A critical task is both high value and time-sensitive.

Section 2 - Chunking Tasks and Building a Schedule

Chunking your time

Chunking your time

Do you ever wish there were more hours in the day? Many people do. They think that having more time means doing more. But personal productivity isn't about putting in more hours on the job. It's about optimizing your work schedule by planning, organizing, and controlling your use of time more effectively.

So perhaps the answer to doing more in the time you have is multitasking – doing more than one thing at a time.

If you've ever had a phone conversation with someone while you're checking your e-mail, or worked on paperwork during a meeting or seminar, then you're multitasking.

In theory, multitasking sounds like it's a good way to boost your efficiency, but in reality it's inefficient. It wastes time, expends energy, and disrupts concentration.

So if multitasking isn't the answer to making the most of your time, what is? The answer is "chunking." Chunking is an organizational strategy for making more efficient use of your time schedule.

Chunking means arranging your schedule so you have segments of time dedicated to one task or type of activity.

Chunking time can boost productivity because focusing on one thing at a time saves the time wasted on task-switching. It can also improve your state of mind, allowing you to concentrate on completing a task in full, and increasing satisfaction with a job well done.

Chunking needs to be done as you're creating your work schedule. Consider what you need to accomplish. If you've kept task logs during the previous week, you'll have a good idea of what you do during a typical week. Group similar tasks and activities together, and then insert chunks of time into your written schedule to do them. Allow at least an hour of uninterrupted time for each chunk to avoid wasting time task-switching.

Group similar tasks and activities together

Each time you shift your attention from one thing to another, you lose focus. And reorienting yourself to the task at hand takes up time. If you group similar tasks or types of activities into the same chunk of time, you'll minimize this time loss. For example, you could cluster together your written correspondence – your e-mail, letters, memos, and reports – and schedule a chunk of time for that purpose. Or if you have regular meetings outside the office, you could schedule them together and save time on travel.

Insert chunks into your written schedule

It's important to include these chunks of time in your written work schedule. Treat them with respect and insert them into your schedule just as you would any other priority item, such as a meeting. When chunks are included in your schedule, they become part of your routine. For example, you could schedule a chunk of time each morning for making personal contact with clients or colleagues.

Schedule at least an hour

You should make sure to schedule at least an hour of uninterrupted time for each chunk in your schedule. Minimize interruptions by explaining to colleagues that you're not available to them during these times. Unless it's necessary to the task at hand, don't check your e-mail and don't answer the phone. You can reply to messages later. If you're polite and consistent in your approach, people will come to accept this time as part of your work routine.

Question

Sales manager Farah is planning her work schedule for the coming week.

How can she apply the strategy of chunking so she uses her time more effectively?

Options:

1. Farah plans all her out of office client meetings for Tuesday and Thursday afternoons

2. Farah incorporates chunks of uninterrupted time into her written schedule

3. Farah includes a three-hour block in her schedule to accommodate her client meetings

4. Farah builds chunks of 15 minutes to half an hour into her schedule

5. Farah uses the first hour of every morning to answer her e-mail while she's meeting with her staff

Answer

Option 1: This option is correct. Successful time chunking involves grouping similar tasks and activities together in the work schedule.

Option 2: This option is correct. It's important that Farah includes chunks of time in her written schedule, just as she would include any other priority item.

Option 3: This option is correct. The most efficient use of time involves scheduling chunks of at least an hour.

Option 4: This option is incorrect. Effective chunking requires you to schedule an hour or more for each chunk of similar or related activities.

Option 5: This option is incorrect. The purpose of chunking is to schedule similar activities together. Trying to do different things at the same time wastes time and reduces concentration because it requires task-switching.

The importance of a written schedule

The importance of a written schedule

Even if you have an excellent memory, it's just not possible to remember everything you have to do every minute of every day. If you don't schedule time for a task, it may not get done. So, once you've set your goals and prioritized your tasks and activities, you'll need to begin properly managing your time. Creating a written schedule will allow you to develop a systematic time frame within which you can efficiently organize everything you need to do.

A schedule is important for personal productivity because it gives you a holistic view of what you need to achieve during a particular period of time.

It also helps you organize your time wisely, allowing enough time to complete important tasks, and preserving time to deal with unexpected situations.

Personal Productivity Improvement

    Scheduling is also valuable because it can keep you from inadvertently double-booking your time, or taking on more commitments than it's possible to handle.

    A written schedule can be created using a paper-based organizer such as a date book, or day planner. Or you may choose a computer or mobile electronic device with scheduling capabilities. Whichever type of scheduler you choose to keep, it should be portable enough to bring with you. You never know when or where you may have to make or reschedule an appointment. You'll save time and minimize errors if you can make those changes immediately.

Principles of scheduling

There are seven basic principles involved in personal scheduling. These principles are to compile the schedule just prior to the period of time covered, begin your schedule with the end in mind, schedule critical tasks first, recognize your controllable time, allow for previously unfinished critical tasks, chunk similar tasks and activities together, and be flexible in your approach.

The first principle of scheduling is that the schedule should be compiled just prior to the period of time it covers.

This helps keep it relevant and eliminates the need for multiple revisions. The time that you choose to cover in your schedule should be dependent on your tasks and the deadlines you have for completing them.

Personal Productivity Improvement

A common length of time for a personal schedule is a week, but if you have more long-term goals your schedule may cover a month or more.

The second principle of scheduling is to begin your schedule with the end in mind. This means starting with the objectives you have to achieve.

Determine what must be finished by the end of each day or week. These are your "deliverables" – time-sensitive tasks that must be completed by a deadline.

For example, you might have to write a proposal or report that has a specific due date. Or perhaps you have to give a presentation, or chair a meeting. Particularly time-sensitive tasks are those where other people are depending on your input so they can complete their own work.

Question
Which are time-sensitive tasks?

Options:
1. Sign paychecks for staff
2. Attend monthly board meeting
3. Research company environmental policy
4. Reorganize filing system

Answer
Option 1: This option is correct. Time-sensitive tasks have a deadline.

Option 2: This option is correct. Time-sensitive tasks are those that you can't put off or delay for long.

Option 3: This option is incorrect. This task may be valuable, but it relates to longer term goals.

Option 4: This option is incorrect. This task doesn't have a deadline.

The third principle of scheduling is to schedule critical-priority tasks first. Critical tasks are those that are both high-value – important to achieving your goals – and time-sensitive. If you've compiled a task list from your task logs, and assessed those tasks with a priority matrix, you'll have identified critical tasks with a number 1. After critical-priority tasks have been scheduled, enter high-priority tasks. Follow this by medium - and – if there's time left – low-priority tasks.

The fourth principle of scheduling is to recognize your controllable time. Now that you've determined what you have to accomplish, it's time to determine how much time you actually have to achieve those objectives. It may be tempting to schedule a full eight hours of vital tasks in every workday, but that's unrealistic. What you'll need to do is determine just how much controllable time you have. That's the time you actually have available to complete your tasks and activities.

To determine your controllable time, think about how many hours there are in your workday. Then consider how much time you spend dealing with unpredictable events. These include routine interruptions such as requests from your boss, phone calls from friends or family, or ad hoc conversations with staff and colleagues.

Unpredictable events also include situations or crises that you have to deal with. For example, you may have to mitigate a disagreement between staff members, or hunt down a new copy of a report that was lost on the way to the printers.

If you keep task logs, this can give you a rough estimate of the time you typically spend dealing with unpredictable events. Deduct this time from your workday, and you'll have your controllable time - the time you actually have to complete your scheduled tasks.

Question

How do you determine your controllable time during a workday?

Options:

1. It's all the time you spend at work
2. Deduct the time you spend dealing with unpredictable events from your total workday
3. Allow an hour each day to deal with unpredictable events

Answer

Option 1: This option is incorrect. To be realistic, you need to allow time for social encounters, crises, or unexpected issues that may take up time during the workday.

Option 2: This is the correct option. Controllable time is the amount of time during the workday that you actually have available to spend completing tasks.

Option 3: This option is incorrect. It's right to allow time for the unpredictable, but you need to study your task logs to determine exactly how much time to allow. No two people have schedules that are exactly the same.

Further principles of scheduling

Further principles of scheduling

The fifth principle of scheduling is to allow time for unfinished critical tasks. Sometimes during the course of your day, you'll encounter issues that are both out of your control and unexpected. This means that no matter how efficiently you plan, you may not always have time to complete critical tasks within your schedule. You'll need "catch-up" time to get back on track.

You may have noted that unexpected but important tasks can include dealing with work crises, client requests, staffing problems, or family emergencies.

For example, a colleague might fail to give you the data you need to compile a critical report. Or the data you need might be lost because of a computer malfunction.

It's important to plan time for unfinished tasks from a previous schedule. This way, you'll keep tasks in priority order and be able to take care of unexpected calls and last minute issues as they arise. If you don't need the time for unfinished critical tasks, you can use it to work ahead on tasks that are high-value but not time-sensitive.

The sixth principle of scheduling is to chunk similar tasks and activities together. You may recall that chunking helps efficiency because it reduces time used task-switching. For example, you may be able to answer a single e-mail in a few minutes, but you may have a dozen or more to get through. It makes sense to group these types of tasks together, rather than waste time switching to and from other kinds of tasks throughout the day.

The seventh principle of scheduling is to be flexible. Your schedule is the ideal organizational plan for the tasks and activities you need to complete. But that doesn't mean it has to be set in stone. Don't be afraid to adjust and readjust your schedule until you have it where you want it.

Think of your schedule as a living document that will evolve through updates and revisions during its lifetime.

For example, what if your boss suddenly changes the regular staff meeting from morning to afternoon? What if a client is delayed in traffic and arrives late for an appointment?

You should be prepared to make changes and rearrange priority items if the need arises. Also, try to schedule more time than you'll need for each task. Leaving a buffer gives you some flexibility in case things take longer than you expected.

Naveen is a client services manager for a national advertising agency. Select each principle of scheduling for an example of how Naveen applies it to his personal schedule.

Compile just prior to time covered

Naveen schedules his time by the week. To make sure his schedules are as current as possible, he includes an hour of uninterrupted time on Friday afternoons to do the next week's schedule.

Begin with the end in mind

Naveen starts with a list of time-sensitive tasks that he knows he'll have to complete during the week. He considers each deadline and assigns the tasks so that deadlines won't be missed.

Schedule critical tasks first

Naveen takes his list of time-sensitive tasks and considers which of them is also of value in achieving his goals. These tasks are rated 1 for critical priority and entered into his schedule first. For example, on Tuesday, Naveen has to meet an important client at the airport at 11:00 a.m. This is a critical task as it can't be delayed and it's valuable to his work.

Recognize controllable time

Naveen estimates that about two hours of his workday are taken up with unpredictable activities such as dealing with coworkers, answering queries from clients, and dealing with crises and issues that arise. Because of this, he allows six hours of controllable time each day in which to pursue the tasks he needs to complete.

Allow for unfinished critical tasks

Naveen allows an hour of flex-time each day to deal with unfinished critical tasks from the

previous day. He builds this into the schedule and uses it if necessary. If not, he works on non- sensitive, high-value tasks such as strategic planning.

Chunk similar tasks and activities

Naveen spends a lot of time compiling customer expectations and requirements for each ad campaign. These are then incorporated into the contract. Naveen allows a 90-minute block each morning to do all his paperwork.

Be flexible

On Tuesday, Naveen readjusts his schedule when his out-of-town client's plane is delayed. He reschedules picking up the client to 1:00 p.m., adds 20 minutes to his travel time to account for traffic, and reschedules his 1:00 p.m. sales call to an open hour at 4:00 p.m.

Question

Greta is an investment specialist with a national bank. She plans her schedule a week at a time.

Which actions illustrate Greta applying the basic principles of scheduling as she plans her week?

Options:

1. Greta plans her upcoming week on the Thursday prior. The first tasks she enters are her meetings with clients.

2. Greta determines her deliverables for each day.

3. Greta allots six hours per day to complete her tasks, and an hour to finish tasks from the previous day.

4. Greta determines her personal contact tasks will take about 45 minutes. So she schedules an hour each day from 3:00 - 4:00 p.m. to return all her calls and e-mail.

5. Greta plans her schedule a month ahead of time. She begins her plans by adding the shortest tasks first.

6. Greta makes sure she has no open time in her schedule in order to maximize her efficiency.

Answer

Option 1: This option is correct. Greta is compiling her schedule just prior to the period of time it covers, and she's covered scheduling critical tasks - those that are both time-sensitive and high-value – first.

Option 2: This option is correct. Greta is beginning with the end in mind. Her deliverables are those time-sensitive tasks that must be finished by a deadline.

Option 3: This option is correct. Greta is recognizing her controllable time and allowing time for unfinished critical tasks.

Option 4: This option is correct. Greta is chunking all her tasks together. She's also being flexible in case her activities take more time than she thinks they will.

Option 5: This option is incorrect. Greta should add the most critical tasks to her schedule first, not the shortest ones. Also, she should be planning her schedule just prior to the time it covers, not a month in advance.

Option 6: This option is incorrect. It's important for Greta to leave time in her schedule to reschedule appointments as needed, and to deal with unexpected events.

Section 3 - Using the To-do List

Types of to-do lists

Types of to-do lists

A to-do list is a simple and commonly used scheduling tool. It captures all the important tasks you need to complete within a given time period. To-do lists usually cover a day, but can cover a week, a month, or any designated time period. A to-do list is compiled with your schedule, and many written and electronic planners have to-do lists built in.

Like schedules, to-do lists contain tasks you need to complete. But to-do lists are different from schedules in that tasks are listed by priority, rather than by time.

When you look over your to-do list, you can assess the tasks in order of priority. Crossing off the tasks on your to-do list can be a great motivator. It's also a good way to monitor your productivity.

Items on your to-do list could include meetings you're scheduled to attend, phone calls you have to make or that you're expecting to receive, written correspondence that has to be completed, and decisions you have to make.

Although daily to-do lists are the most common type, to-do lists can serve different purposes. Some businesspeople keep different to-do lists to serve the different functions they have to fulfill. Types of to-do lists include the daily to-do list, the projects to-do list, and the long-term to-do list.

Daily

The daily to-do list is a list of action items to be completed within a business day. For example, some people create their to-do list from their schedules, others create the list first and use it to complete their schedules each day.

Project

A project to-do list itemizes the actions needed to meet deadlines and milestones for a specific project or initiative. This type of to-do list can help you plan a long-term schedule more efficiently.

Long-term

A long-term to-do list itemizes the tasks that are valuable for working toward your goals, but aren't time-sensitive. These may be tasks you want to do at some point, but don't have the time or resources to pursue at the present time. The long-term to-do list is useful as a reference when you find you have some time on your hands and can afford to work ahead on long-term goals.

Different people can use to-do lists in different ways in different situations. For instance, if you're in sales, you might want to use your to-do list to focus on tasks that help meet short-term sales targets.

If you work in strategic or operational planning, you'll probably be focusing on much longer-term goals.

To-do lists also help maintain your work-life balance. Some people maintain a personal to-do list alongside a business list. Other people combine the two to create a balanced "life list."

Characteristics of effective to-do lists

Characteristics of effective to-do lists

An effective to-do list has three basic characteristics. It should be written down – whether on paper or in electronic format. It should be short – preferably ten items or fewer. And the tasks should be prioritized by importance.

Written down

Very few people can keep an accurate to-do list in their memory. Writing down your list and crossing off items will make sure it's accurate and up-to-date. This can be accomplished by a simple written list, or by entering the information into an electronic device.

Short

An ideal to-do list should contain only about ten items. Trying to add too many tasks could overwhelm you and set you up for failure. You could think about your to-do list as a "top ten" list with the ten most valuable things you have to get done. Add critical items first, then include lower priority items as long as the list has room.

Prioritized by importance

The primary purpose of a to-do list isn't to get everything done. It's to make sure that your most valuable tasks are completed. That's why to-do lists are prioritized. Prioritizing your list identifies which are the most important items in your schedule, and which can be postponed if necessary.

Prioritized by importance

The primary purpose of a to-do list isn't to get everything done. It's to make sure that your most valuable tasks are completed. That's why to-do lists are prioritized. Prioritizing your list identifies which are the most important items in your schedule, and which can be postponed if necessary.

Prioritized by importance

The primary purpose of a to-do list isn't to get everything done. It's to make sure that your most valuable tasks are completed. That's why to-do lists are prioritized. Prioritizing your list identifies which are the most important items in your schedule, and which can be postponed if necessary.

People use different designations and different levels of assessment for prioritizing tasks. Some classify tasks simply as urgent, or not urgent. Others may use A, B, C, D, or 1, 2, 3, or use colors. Some people have a designation system unique to themselves. But however you designate priority, you'll need to make sure the most critical tasks go at the top of your to-do list with the others in descending order of importance.

Question

Personal Productivity Improvement

Benji is a sales manager for an auto dealership. He creates a daily to-do list from his schedule each morning. Which characteristics make Benji's list an effective to-do list?

A laptop computer with a to do list on the screen. The four list items are:

Priority A. Compile sales report.
Priority A. Send sales report to head office.
Priority A. Sign contract for new ad campaign.
Priority B. Review specifications for new car models.

Options:

1. Benji keeps his list recorded in his laptop
2. Benji prioritizes his list with the most urgent tasks at the top
3. Benji lists no more than four or five items at a time to ensure he completes the list each day
4. Benji includes only critical priority items on his daily to-do lists

Answer

Option 1: This option is correct. An effective to-do list is written down.

Option 2: This option is correct. An effective to-do list prioritizes tasks by importance.

Option 3: This option is incorrect. Benji's daily to-do list would have been more effective if he'd had about ten items.

Option 4: This option is incorrect. Critical priority items are listed first on an effective to-do list, but lower priority items should be included as long as the list has room.

Making effective use of to-do lists

Making effective use of to-do lists

Putting together a properly structured to-do list seems simple. However, there are five simple guidelines that can help you use to-do lists more effectively. The guidelines are to break items down into achievable tasks, create realistic objectives and time lines, assign priorities to list items, revise the list as needed, and keep motivated.

The first guideline for using to-do lists effectively is to break items down into achievable tasks. Keep in mind that your schedule and your to-do list work together, but they serve different purposes. Not every task in your schedule is in a suitable form for adding to your to-do list. Complicated, loosely defined, or time-consuming activities will need to be broken down into smaller tasks.

For example, say you have a scheduled task like "Do project progress report." You could break that task into smaller, achievable tasks. Think about what doing the report entails. You have to collect data, interpret the results, write your conclusions, format the report, and e-mail it to your boss. If that report is due on Friday, you could start on Monday, and add one task to your to-do list each day.

The second guideline for using to-do lists effectively is to create realistic and achievable objectives that can be completed within a reasonable time frame. Make sure you don't have too many items, or not enough. It's rewarding to be able to cross an item off your to-do list and know that you've made real progress toward achieving your goals. But it's hard to know what you've achieved if a list item is vague, lacks definition, or is too subjective.

To-do list items need to tell you at a glance exactly what needs doing. This means they need to contain specific action verbs, and to contain the criteria you'll use to measure whether the task has been completed.

For example, "Inspire team to work harder" isn't an appropriate item for a to-do list because you have no way to tell when or if you've achieved your objective.

A better to-do list item would be something like "Prepare a 20-minute presentation on 'meeting objectives' for Friday staff meeting." This item is specific, measurable, and actionable.

Time lines are also important. When you're considering a task, think about how much time it will take, and make sure you've allowed enough time in your schedule.

If the task seems overwhelming, consider whether there are elements of that task that could be deferred to another day, or delegated to someone else.

Then you can concentrate on the achievable elements of the task.

Question

Which items might belong on an effective to-do list?

Options:

1. Print out ten copies of project report
2. E-mail Frank re signing his contract
3. Keep Mr. Anderson happy
4. Get in touch with team member

Answer

Option 1: This option is correct. This list item is specific about what needs to be achieved.

Option 2: This option is correct. An effective to-do list item is specific and achievable.

Option 3: This option is incorrect. This list item is too subjective. Effective list items are objective and specific.

Option 4: This option is incorrect. This item isn't specific enough to be an effective list item. It should include the person's name, and the method of contact.

The third guideline for using to-do lists effectively is to assign priorities to your list items.

Remember that an effective to-do list prioritizes tasks in order of importance. This doesn't mean that you have to do the tasks in order, but it does remind you of your most critical tasks each time you look at the list.

You can list your to-do items in order of priority, or chronologically as they appear in your schedule. The important thing is that you have a clear system for assigning priorities to each item.

When you were building your schedule, you may have used a priority matrix to assess the importance of your tasks. This is also a good tool to use with your to-do list. The most common method is to designate priority using numbers. Use 1 for critical tasks, those that are time-sensitive and high value. Use 2 for high – high value but not time-sensitive. Use 3 for medium – time-sensitive, but low value, and use 4 for low – neither time-sensitive nor high value.

Flexibility and motivation

Flexibility and motivation

The fourth guideline for using to-do lists effectively is to revise your list as needed. To be effective, the to-do list must be current. And for that reason, you must be prepared to review and amend your to-do list regularly. You should be ready to make ongoing changes based on completed tasks, revised deadlines, and unpredictable events.

For example say you're interrupted by a crisis – your boss wants you to come to the senior staff meeting, take notes, and prepare a briefing for your department that afternoon. It's time to return to your to-do list, evaluate where you stand, and revise the list as needed. Since your boss's request has become your top priority, you can drop the lowest priority tasks from your list. These tasks can be added to the next day's to-do list.

Personal Productivity Improvement

The fifth guideline for using to-do lists effectively is to keep motivated. If you knew that by finishing all your tasks by the end of the day, you'd get a cash reward, or time off from work, would you be motivated to check things off your list? It's more than likely you would. How efficient and effective you are in doing your job has as much to do with motivation as it does with meticulous scheduling.

Keeping motivated means not losing faith in your own ability to make time work for you or to see your tasks through.

One of the best ways to stay strong in your belief in yourself is to keep track of your successes, even the small ones.

When you're feeling down on yourself, go back to your schedules and to-do lists and remind yourself of how much you've accomplished.

But don't push so hard that your personal life suffers. Overwork and fatigue can easily demotivate you. Remember that working efficiently doesn't mean you have to work long hours or late into the night. It means organizing your time to produce the most value in the time you have available.

Once you've finished a task, you can also keep motivated by rewarding yourself for a job well done. This doesn't have to be a big reward. It can be as simple as taking a coffee break or spending some time on a more enjoyable task.

Anna is a manager at a large public relations company. Anna makes effective use of a daily to-do list by breaking items down, creating realistic objectives, assigning priorities, revising as needed, and keeping herself motivated.

Break items down

Anna notes that she has an hour set aside for paperwork. For her to-do list, she looks at each sub-task in this hour and determines that preparing the contract for CrossCountry Airways is time-sensitive and high value. Anna adds this to the list.

Create realistic objectives

Anna reviews her tasks to make sure they are worded in an objective and achievable manner. She considers the list item "Finish contract" and revises it to "Proof and approve contract for CrossCountry Airways by noon."

Assign priorities

Anna checks her schedule for the next day and lists all the critical tasks. She then lists the high, medium, and low priority tasks.

Revise as needed

Anna compiles her list by adding her top ten most important tasks for the day. At 10:00 a.m., her boss calls and asks to reschedule their weekly meeting to the next day, Anna reschedules the meeting and moves a lower priority item onto her task list to fill the spot.

Keep motivated

Anna crosses each task off her list as she completes it. By the end of the working day, she's completed all of the items on her list, and leaves the office well ahead of her less efficient colleagues.

Question

Reg is the manager of a large shopping complex. Each evening, Reg compiles a to-do list from his next day's schedule. He revises it again the next morning after he

Personal Productivity Improvement

checks his messages. Through the day, Reg crosses off items as he completes them. He often works far into the evening to complete each item on his list.

How could Reg improve his use of to-do lists?

A to-do list with ten tasks.

1 Prepare agenda for Merchants' Association meeting.
1 Meeting with Merchants' Association Board.
1 Send sales report to head office.
1 Meet with potential new merchant
(Joyce James - Bloom's Flowers).
2 Paperwork.
2 Book portable stage for spring fashion show.
2 Sign renewal of contract for kiosk rental.
(Priya Smith).
2 Send notice re overdue rent to Brocadero Shoes.
3 Attend Chamber of Commerce luncheon.
4 Coffee with Jane in Food Court.

Options:

1. Reg's list items should be more specific
2. Reg needs to keep motivated
3. Reg could prioritize the high value tasks
4. Reg could start with more items on his list

Answer

Option 1: This option is correct. The list item "Paperwork" isn't a realistic objective because it isn't specific enough to be achieved and crossed off the list.

Option 2: This option is correct. One purpose of a to-do list is to motivate yourself to be more productive so you can enjoy the time you save. Reg needs to learn to enjoy his time, and move unfinished items to the next day's list.

Option 3: This option is incorrect. Reg assigns the time-sensitive and high value tasks a one and puts them at the top of his list.

Option 4: This option is incorrect. Ten items is a realistic number for a daily to-do list. And completing his list will be more motivating than not completing a longer list.

REFERENCES

References
1. **Organizing Your Workspace: A Guide to Personal Productivity, Revised Edition** - 1999, Odette Pollar, Crisp Learning
2. **Make Every Second Count: Time Management Tips and Techniques for More Success with Less Stress** - 2010, Robert W. Bly, Career Press
3. **Time Power: A Proven System for Getting More Done in Less Time Than You Ever Thought Possible** - 2004, Brian Tracy
4. **How to Manage Your Priorities, Second Edition** - 2007, Janis Fisher Chan
5. **Make Every Second Count: Time Management Tips and Techniques for More Success with Less Stress** - 2010, Robert W. Bly, Career Press
6. **Time Management: Increase Your Personal Productivity and Effectiveness** -

2005, Harvard Business School (Ed.), Harvard Business School Press
7. **Taking Control with Time Management, Fourth Edition** - 1998, MJ Weeks
8. **Focus Like a Laser Beam: 10 Ways to Do What Matters Most** - 2006, Lisa Haneberg, Jossey-Bass

www.ingramcontent.com/pod-product-compliance
Lightning Source LLC
Chambersburg PA
CBHW020915180526
45163CB00007B/2740